CW00802082

THE DIARY OF A
GATEKEEPER

DAVID WALTHER

Second Edition published 2019
2QT Limited (Publishing)
Settle, North Yorkshire BD24 9RH United Kingdom

First edition published by Balboa Press

The author has his own website: www.davidwalther.co

Cover illustrations by Matt Brown.

This story is woven together from some events that are real but might seem unreal
and some events that are unreal but might seem real. Any resemblance to persons and
places you know is entirely coincidental.

Printed By Amazon

A CIP catalogue record for this book is available
from the British Library
ISBN 978-1-913071-29-5

For all those beautiful people who have helped me develop
over the years, including the ones who do not know it
And to my author mentor Tom Evans for his invaluable
help and assistance in producing this book

In a far off plain, resident in the spirit realm for those with eyes that could see, was a sight to behold. The air crackled with explosive potential. Two opposing forces faced one another across a dark grey landscape set on a green plain of grass. One of light, one of dark.

On each side, lines of beings, numbering in their thousands, stared across the battle field to come.

Dark forces from the underworld with malevolence and snarls. Noises that made your skin crawl for those with ears to hear.

Light forces stared back with resolution, their determination and strength no less fierce than their counterparts across the still fresh green grass. At the head of each army stood one solitary figure.

Archangel Michael, glowing blue. His hand on the hilt of his sword, reflecting the colour and glow of its owner.

Lucifer, Lord of the Underworld. Deepest darkest black. Hand on his own black sword hilt.

Their eyes locked while three beings of power watched from above.

PREFACE

On first reading, you may think this book is a work of fiction. This is completely understandable, as events described here sound fantastical and other-worldly. Insofar as the minds and experiences of the protagonists are concerned at the very least, they all happened. Naturally, they may have been imagined. If so, they were collectively imagined by all the parties present. The physical world we experience is the tip of a multi-dimensional iceberg. Most peoples' experiences of other planes of being come in the form of dreams and daydreams. These days we largely assume that all things mystical, as depicted in films, on TV, and in books, are fairy tales and nonsense.

Our scientists are the new wizards. They can explain everything. We are the lords of the physical plane. As we come to understand the physical plane in more and more detail, it has a tendency to densify. This causes energies trapped on the earth plane to be forced out of the cracks. These energies can be confused and bewildered and in need of help.

The experiences of the medium, Mark Ash, recounted here show us that what we think of as our reality is a thinly veiled illusion. Our world is no more than a consensual dream. What happens when other planes intersect with it looks like magic, witchcraft, and sorcery.

Some sensitives can both perceive and communicate with these other worlds when they impact and impinge on ours. They are the gatekeepers and the guardians.

Note that all books and films that describe magic are imbued with some of that same magic and energy. For this reason, this book is charged with a special energy and a form of spell. Some readers may begin to spontaneously experience similar events, so this book contains protective energy and symbology, such that only spirits with positive intent can appear through the veil.

Although this book describes the dispelling of dark energies, the light is much stronger and will always prevail. In fact, even the darkest dark has an inkling of light within.

Nothing real can be destroyed. Nothing unreal can persist. All is real in some form.

CHAPTER 1

THE MEETING

Medium [noun]: A person who acts as a conduit between two worlds. Mediums receive messages from spirit guides and discarnate souls and relay them to the earth plane. Some mediums work verbally, some with music, and some via art. They also are known as channels.

Clearing [Noun]: Generic term referring to the removal of entities and such from premises.

It had been the usual kind of afternoon for Mark Ash that Friday back in May. He had been working upstairs in Steel's House in the main therapy room. Business was usually good, situated as it was in a quaint English northern town. It was one of the few therapy rooms available for many miles around. The afternoon had gone smoothly enough. He'd seen several clients for healing and had slipped in a few clairvoyant readings as well.

Later on he was planning to attend his monthly Platform Mediumship event with fellow mediums Susan Wright and Peter Crowley. At these events, the mediums relayed messages from within the spirit realms to the audience. These messages could be from their own personal spirit guides, the guides of the audience, ancestors who had passed over, or anything else from the spirit world. The event always brought some surprises.

So it was that, after getting off work in town, Mark found himself taking the short walk to the usual venue. He looked forward to the evening as he entered the main event room, a rectangular hall about twenty-five metres long by ten metres wide. It was part of a council building used for all kinds of events. The room had all the usual amenities, including a bar next door that sold drinks. As a result, there was always a residual smell of beer hanging around. That evening, though, alcohol was off limits; just glasses and jugs of water sat on a table near the entrance for all to help themselves.

Despite the beer smell, the hall had a nice airy feel with a positive energy. Large open windows adorned one wall, and bright abstract pictures the others. Chairs sat in neat rows, with a table at the front holding flickering candles and small crystal statues. The usual forty or so people had turned up. Most were familiar faces, but some new ones were in attendance too. The numbers had risen steadily since their small beginnings a year ago. Now the word was getting out in the surrounding area. Quite a buzz filled the room that night, both from the earthly throng and from the various spirits and guides who had popped along to share their wisdom and, in some cases, just to reassure loved ones that all was well.

Mark always supplied a display of crystals at these events. He didn't bring them just to sell. They also enhanced the energy of the room for both spirit and the attendees, and they eased the pathways for cross-communication. His table full of beautiful crystals had attracted the lion's share of attention that night, and he was glad that Sonia, a close friend, had turned up to help—especially because he would have to disappear and prepare with the other mediums about fifteen minutes prior to the event starting.

The evening went well. Marie, Susan's sister—a sensitive herself—acted as host. After offering the introductions, Marie concluded by mentioning that the mediums would be available to be spoken to personally at the end of the meeting. An hour or so later, after he finished his channelling session on stage, Mark made his way back to his table and was pleased to see his stock of crystals was down by more than 50 per cent. Some decent sales had occurred that night.

When the final medium had finished, Marie encouraged the audience to find the medium they were most drawn to for a longer chat and perhaps to book a private reading if they so wished. Mark seemed especially popular that evening. Just when he'd finished talking to the queue of people who'd attended his crystal display, a tall, slim, demure Indian woman approached him. She had been hovering in the background, waiting for a chance to speak to him.

'Hi, I'm Anya,' she said with a smile as she proffered her hand.

Mark took her delicate hand and shook it gently. 'Hi, Anya, how can I help?'

'Well,' she replied, 'I have been having a problem in my house. There is a nasty spirit in there causing us a lot of problems.'

'Okay, how do you know that?'

'I can sense these things. I'm from India originally, and a Hindu, so I can pick up on things going on in the house. And it's not just me sensing things either.'

Mark nodded to give encouragement. This sounded right up his street.

'My eldest daughter is very spiritual, you know, and she feels things too. Actually, I have twins—two girls—but I always call her my eldest because she came first. She doesn't feel safe in her bedroom and is now sleeping with me. I'm concerned for her safety—and the rest of us also. Objects are being moved in the house. Some are not found for days; others just disappear, even though I know exactly where I put them. And it's not just my things that are being moved. Others' are too.' Anya looked more deeply into Mark's eyes. 'We've been having money problems for a while now, and business deals keep dropping through for both my husband and me. Household bills and general maintenance costs are increasing, because things break and the car keeps going wrong. It's like a continuous run of bad luck and ill fortune, but I know it's not. It's more than that. The whole family feels uncomfortable in our house now.'

'Hmmm,' he said. 'That is strange.'

Still fully connected to spirit as a result of his earlier performance, Mark knew something was definitely up with this situation and that Anya and her family had a problem that wasn't just a run of bad luck. Conscious that the choice had to be hers, he paused a second and resumed clearing away his crystals so he could be out of the room by 9:30 p.m. He decided to leave it to spirit and her to decide.

He turned back to Anya and said, 'Okay. Well, either Susan or I can help you for sure. Just go with who feels right to you, and that will be the right choice.'

Anya didn't hesitate. She looked at him earnestly. 'I do like Susan, but I am drawn to you. You are the one who is meant to help me.'

Instinctively, he sensed she was correct.

'Okay, here's my card. Why don't you give me a call in the next day or so, and we'll talk further? I can definitely help you with this, so don't worry anymore,' he said with a smile.

'Thank you, Mark. I'll call you tomorrow to arrange to see you.' With a final smile, Anya turned away, looking at the business card she now held in her hand.

Mark took his leave of Marie and Susan and quickly finished packing away for the night. He was looking forward to Anya calling him. There was something intriguing about her, and he was sure he would hear from her soon.

Sure enough, a few days later he did so. She contacted him by email, reminding him of their chat. He made an appointment to visit her home a few days later, and he assured her that if there was anything in her house that shouldn't be, he would remove it and leave the house clear and cleansed of negative energy.

The day before he was due to attend to her house, he received a worried phone call. 'Hi, Mark. It's Anya.'

'Hi, Anya. How are you?'

'I'm good, thanks. Mark, I'm worried about this session, with you coming over. Can you tell me what's going to happen please?'

'Sure. I won't know exactly what I'll need to do until I arrive and have a look around, but in essence, I will come over, feel the energy of the house, see what's going on, and pick up anything that is there. Then I'll deal with it.'

'How long will it take?'

'That varies, but I've never taken longer than four or five hours to do a large five-bedroom house. It may take less time, but I won't leave without completing the job. To be honest, I'd rather not do it than leave it incomplete. It's not like I'm decorating and can come back the next day to finish painting a wall. I won't leave until I'm satisfied it is safe and the energy of the house is good.'

'Oh, okay.'

'Don't worry. I will be completely straight with you. You won't get overcharged, and I won't stay there any longer than I have to. But I will stay until it's finished and I'm happy. That's a condition of me doing the entity clearing, Anya. Otherwise, I would not be able to come.'

Her answer surprised him. 'That's okay, Mark. I trust you. That's why I came to you in the first place. I have already tuned in to you. I know more about you than you realize!'

5

CHAPTER 2

FIRST CONTACT

Chakra [noun]: A bidirectional energy vortex by which the physical and ethereal planes intercommunicate and transfer energy. There are seven main chakras and over two hundred minor chakras on the normal human body, and several above and below the physical form.

Cleansing [noun]: A term used to describe the removal of negative energies, replacing them with positive. This typically occurs in a residence, and is especially important after an entity has been removed.

The appointment was confirmed for midday. Mark only took a couple of things with him—some sage and a Tibetan metal singing bowl for cleansing negative energy, both wrapped up securely in the boot of his car. Good preparation prior to arrival at a house clearing was essential.

Methodically, he prepared mentally, bringing down some initial protection of light to surround himself, encasing both his physical and ethereal body completely. He closed his chakras and asked his spirit guides to step in closer to help. They knew what was happening, of course, and were there with him as always, but it was still nice to ask for help. They appreciate a polite request, and it opens up a clearer line of communication.

Mark turned into Anya's private road, which was situated in an affluent residential area with a collection of large detached houses, and spotted Anya's house. He parked the car just outside, switched the engine off, and sat for a moment to settle down and focus his thoughts to the task ahead. Some minutes later he exited his car and took stock of Anya's property. It was a modern five-bedroom house with a double garage, and it couldn't have been more than ten years old. Situated in a spacious plot of land with large gardens, it boasted a long drive way flanked by lawns on either side. Three exotic cars were parked in the driveway.

Mark gathered his small bag from the boot and then approached the house and knocked on the door. It was opened within seconds by an expectant Anya.

She gave him a warm infectious smile and invited him in through the hallway into her cloakroom-cum-study. He placed his coat and tools on top of the desk by the far wall. Immediately his guides, who had come in force, moved around the house, placing themselves at strategic locations to manipulate the energies. This would secure and prevent anything non-physical from leaving or entering. After exchanging pleasantries with Anya for a few minutes, he decided the best thing to do was to start by looking around, and he suggested that Anya should leave him to it.

He walked into the living room, a large space with a brown patterned carpet and an authentic antique Indian feel to it. This room opened up into a modern open-plan dining area via a wide walkthrough, creating a generous and spacious feel. A further door opened on the left into a large kitchen. A sizeable wooden dining table took centre stage in the dining room, with an old fashioned sideboard flanking the far wall. In the living area was some old-style furniture, and Indian-themed adornments were hanging on the walls.

7

Mark pulled out a decorative wooden chair from under the main table in the dining room, and sat down to meditate.

Once he had relaxed, Mark slowed his breathing, taking long deep breaths, then fully exhaling and pausing without inhaling for several seconds. He did this to slow his body down and clear his mind. Then he sent his energy down through his feet into the ground, travelling through the depths of the earth right to the centre, penetrating all layers like giant roots anchoring and grounding him. This was important to stabilise his energy while he sent his spirit up to access the higher levels, which was required for what he was about to do.

He cleared his mind and felt his inner sense heighten and tune in to the energies of the house. Then, pulling down white light from above, he encased himself in a powerful protective bubble to shield him from any negative energies or entities that might be there, and he called in his guides and various spiritual helpers to support and protect him.

Suddenly he became aware of a presence above him. While he honed in, he looked up, using his spirit eyes, and saw a distorted malevolent face peering straight at him through the ceiling just a few feet above where he sat. The head appeared considerably larger than that of an average human, with large bulging eyes, each of different size. The mouth looked like a twisted gash, with a lolling tongue and dripping spittle. Large misshapen teeth and protruding lips of differing thickness were pulled into a grimace. It stared at him with malevolent curiosity, its eyes surveying the scene.

As comprehension slowly dawned as to Mark's purpose, its malevolent curiosity rapidly transformed to outright hostility and aggression. The grotesque face leaned even closer to Mark and actually increased in size, the expression becoming one of anger and outrage. Its eyes bulged, and its mouth gaped even more, showing large yellow-stained teeth.

Mark sat in the chair, calm and confident in his power and levels of protection. As he looked at the grotesque entity with spiritual eyes, Mark sent a mental message. *'I am not afraid, and you will be leaving here soon.'*

With a wicked scowl the head withdrew, retreating through the ceiling to the rear right-hand corner of the house, just above the patio doors that led to the garden. Mark got up and went to Anya in her study and asked, 'What's in that area upstairs above the patio door leading to the garden?'

'That's Sarah's room. Why?'

'Because there's something up there.'

Then he went upstairs to investigate.

CHAPTER 3

HIDING

Entity [noun]: A thought form or collection of thought forms, which acts as a sink for similar thought forms such that it reaches a critical mass and can then leak energy back into the earth plane. They can be hundreds or even thousands of years old. Although they can be frightening, they only have power over us if they are given power.

M ark climbed the carpeted stairs to the main landing. He felt a slight change when he reached the top step. The landing was large and wide for an upstairs area, and various rooms led off it. He looked to the left and entered what he now knew to be the eldest daughter's bedroom. This was the room he had seen the entity withdraw to. Immediately, he felt a coldness in the room, an empty unwelcome feeling, not too strong but definitely there. He walked around for a minute or so without noticing anything too obvious, but these creatures are not stupid. They will hide if they feel it's prudent and wait for him to leave.

He pulled out an office chair from under the desk against the wall, sat in the middle of the room, and focused his attention, pulling in energy from all around and speaking to his guides.

They gathered around, supporting and lending their strength to his, as they spread around the room. Then he sensed it.

It appeared seemingly out of nowhere, and it moved towards him with tangible evil intent. With a reflex action, Mark drew in his protective shield and stood up, lifting his hands, instantly shooting energy from them towards it, encircling and restraining it and preventing any chance of escape. Immobilised, the malevolent being roared. It immediately resisted, pushing against the bonds that held it captive. Mark called his spirit guides for more help.

'Time for you to leave,' he said out loud. Mark called down a portal of light into the room and asked for any of its relatives, friends, or spiritual guardians to support and encourage him.

Gently pushing the entity towards the beckoning portal, he again asked it to leave. Its struggles increased in tempo as it pulled hard against the energy bonds that held it in place. He repeated his command for it to leave, tightening his grip but still trying to be gentle, and pushed it towards the portal, with his guides lending their strength, encircling and moving it closer. The being was drawn inexorably towards the light, kicking and screaming. It pulled against them until the last moment. Then it was suddenly over, and the entity disappeared. The resistance was gone.

Mark paused and took a moment to check, extending his senses out. He could not feel or see it any longer, but then he noticed another spirit across the landing in another room. It had the form of a young boy. Unsure at first, he immediately put up an energy wall of light around the room, and his guides stationed themselves around, sealing him in. He would deal with the boy later.

Something nagged at him, but he couldn't quite put his finger on it. With a final quick glance around the room, he took a deep breath and went downstairs, entering the study where Anya was working on her laptop. He told her what he'd been doing and what had happened, and she listened intently. The she got him a glass of water. Gratefully, he drank a few mouthfuls and then went back upstairs to set about finishing the cleansing and dealing with the young boy who was still up there.

On re-entering the eldest daughter's bedroom, he sat down in the centre to make sure everything was okay and started the cleansing process. He checked behind him and saw that the young boy was still in the room, contained and not causing any problems.

Then he sensed something. Tuning in his senses, he felt … something. A suspicion formed in his mind, which seconds later became stark reality. The entity was still here!

Spirits and entities are not stupid. Some can be just like parasites, a virus almost. They hide in the corners of rooms, behind things, feeding from positive energy with little thought. However, just like in the physical world, different levels of entities and spirits exhibit different amounts of intelligence and cunning. This one had tried to trick him and had kept a large part of its essence hidden, allowing only a smaller part to be sent away in an effort to evade capture.

Mark stepped away from the chair and stood in the centre of the room. He pulled down a bubble of protective light around him and called his most powerful guides and Archangel Michael to come in close again. He had tried asking nicely and offering love, but these methods hadn't succeeded in moving the core of the entity into the portal. A more direct approach was required. When he focused intensely, bright white light shot out from his upraised hands, encircling and restraining the entity, forcing it towards the white circular portal which suddenly appeared a few feet to his right, where it had been summoned by Mark's guides.

The guides had their hands full also in assisting and pulling this monstrosity. It is in our nature to move spirits and entities on with love and kindness, being as gentle as possible, but this was proving all but impossible in this case. This was such a malicious spirit—digging its spiritual heels down with all its might. It had no intent of moving if it could avoid it.

Mark had dealt with many malicious spirits in his time, but this was by far the strongest and nastiest. With a frown of concentration, he summoned yet more power. Then he increased the light and energy directed at it and forced the entity towards the portal.

The entity screamed in rage like some wild, demented banshee. It twisted and turned with every essence of its being in an effort to resist its inexorable journey towards the portal, but slowly Mark was winning the battle. After a minute or two of struggle, with one last heave and blast of light, it was pushed through and disappeared. A fraction of a second later the portal winked shut. Drawing a deep breath, Mark relaxed. An immediate feeling of lightness entered the room, and the tangible heaviness, which moments before had pervaded the room, lifted.

He felt drained. For a few moments he stood there, waiting and feeling the energy in the room to be sure it was gone. He asked his guides, and they confirmed it had. He glanced behind him and noticed that the boy was still contained in the other room across the landing. The lad wasn't causing any problems, just standing there surrounded by the energy wall and guides. Satisfied, Mark made his way downstairs and went back to Anya's study. He slumped wearily in the chair opposite her.

CHAPTER 4

THE BOY

Portal [noun]: A thin place which allows entry and exit of the earth plane for spirit energies and thought forms. Some portals are open all the time, and these tend to be at the confluence of lay lines. Some open spontaneously, while others have to be coaxed in and out of existence.

Gateway [noun]: Similar to a portal, but tends to be used for more benign beings ready to move on to the light, whereas Portals are most often used for connections to the Underworld and less enlightened levels. In truth, though, it's just name play; both provide access from the physical to the spiritual realms at the appropriate level.

Mark reached for the glass of water which still sat on the table in front of him and took a few deep swallows while Anya looked on. He gathered his thoughts and proceeded to give her a synopsis of the events upstairs. Her eyes widened as the tale unfolded. Ten minutes later, feeling his energy return, he made his way back upstairs, telling Anya he would return when he'd finished.

At the top of the stairs, immediately on his right, stood the bedroom where he had left the boy spirit secured. When he approached the doorway he could see him just standing there. Around nine years old, he was a small boy of slight build in grey shorts and shirt, similar to a traditional school uniform. He was just standing by a desk being quiet.

Mark entered the room. As he walked through the surrounding energy walls, he left them intact, as he didn't want to be chasing this spirit all over the house. The young boy just watched him. He seemed to be minding his own business, keeping himself to himself, aware Mark was there but doing nothing. Mark decided to ask him some questions to find out who he was and why he was here.

'Hello,' he said in his mind, '*Who are you?*' Mark's guides were behind him, lending their support and insight and helping Mark to communicate with this boy spirit. The boy did not reply. '*What are you doing here?*'

'*I used to live here.*' The young boy replied in a surprisingly adult voice considering his physical appearance. '*I died in this house.*'

If that was true, it would explain why he was in the house. Mark knew that when the young depart early, they often have an attachment to the physical realms and get stuck in an earthbound state. Caught in the trauma of his physical experience as a boy, he would be unable to move on into the spirit realms. He was trapped between two planes of existence and was effectively haunting the earthly plane.

But Mark could tell he was not being wholly truthful. Spirits who are not out for the highest good are prone not to be. This boy wasn't a relative of current or previous occupants. On further questioning, it turned out he was just interested in the house and what was going on inside, so he had joined in. He was being generally mischievous, moving objects around and upsetting the balance of the house. It was obvious he thought this was fun, as a naughty boy of his apparent age well might.

Mark realised the boy was no real danger, but his mischievous nature would cause further problems if he was allowed to stay, so he asked for a gateway to be brought down to help the spirit cross over. When the opening appeared in the room close to him, the young boy turned and looked. It was golden and beckoned with a bright warm glow, pulling the boy towards it. Mark offered encouragement and gently pushed him towards the circle of light. The boy reached the edge without pausing and then stepped through and disappeared, crossing over to the non-physical realm. The gateway vanished instantly behind him.

Mark stood for a moment, again extending his senses out to check if he had really gone or not. This time he knew. It felt right. The energy was lighter, and a feeling of peace came down. His guides confirmed that the boy had indeed gone. It was now time to cleanse the house of all residue and negative energy and finish the job.

His mind made up, Mark walked downstairs and popped his head into Anya's study where she was still sitting at her desk, typing away on her laptop. Mark explained what he had done and that, now both spirits were gone, he needed to cleanse the house. It would involve going into each room and pulling down positive cleansing energy and light into the area. He explained that he would use the Tibetan singing bowl and burning sage, filling the house with incense. Afterwards she could open all the windows to clear it out, but it might smell of sage for a while. Anya agreed.

It is incredibly important to cleanse a house of any residual energy the spirits may have left behind. These types of energies, if not cleared, will leave the house still feeling uncomfortable and will bring the occupants' mood down. This tends to leave them feeling unhappy which, in turn, brings in new negative energies. Such negative energies tend to gather in corners and behind furniture, TVs, and computers where the air doesn't circulate much.

He started with the lounge. Pulling out a chair again, he sat and took deep breaths and relaxed, focusing his intention and power. Next, he summoned beautiful bright white light from the universe above and all around him and pulled it down. The light cascaded from above like a heavy shower over the whole house, travelling through the roof, rather than bouncing off it. Every room, every corner, every centimetre was touched and absorbed.

He watched the process, feeling it, making sure the light went everywhere, with no stone unturned and no corner empty. The light also cleansed him, and he gave an involuntary shiver of delight from the tingling sensation as it coursed through him.

That was the foundation of the cleanse, which he repeated in each room. On entering each one, he stood in the centre and again pulled down the white light, looking around the room, checking that each corner and hidden area was bathed in the beautiful light, cleansing and purifying all negative residues. The rivers of light surrounding him installed a sense of peace, allowing him to concentrate on doing the job.

Once he had completed the light cleansing, Mark took the staircase to the downstairs cloakroom and collected the Tibetan singing bowl he had brought. He began in the cloakroom-cum-study, and walked around, holding the bowl on a small ornate pad in his left hand, the striker in his right. He moved the edge of the striker around the outer lip of the bowl several times, causing it to develop a constant reverberating sound, which built up in intensity until it reached maximum vibration as he walked around the lounge.

Mark lifted the bowl towards the ceiling, right into the corners of the room. He walked round the outer edges of the room methodically—behind furniture, TVs, music systems, window edges, and all doorways—covering the centre also. Next, he moved into the dining area and repeated the process. He repeated these actions in all the rooms and walking areas in the house, both upstairs and downstairs, careful to miss nothing. As he did so, he spoke in quiet but powerful tones, lending the power of intention to the cleansing process.

'I cleanse this room of all negative energy.'

On entering the eldest daughter's bedroom, he paid particular attention to the process. He intensified his thoughts and intention, making sure he removed all negative residue of the spirit that had resided here. Then he moved into the bedroom where the young boy had been and repeated the procedure, keeping focused and intense. He wanted no residue of either spirit left in the house. Satisfied, Mark went downstairs and sat in front of Anya again.

CHAPTER 5

CLEANSING

Thought forms [noun]: Thoughts don't become things; they are things. Enough of the same type of thought manifests as energy, which can then influence matters and events on the earth plane. Thought forms consist of feelings of kindness, happiness, and creativity, as well as those of grief, sadness, guilt, and fear. Like all energy, they can be focused, directed, manipulated, and annulled.

Mark's shoulders slumped slightly. His fatigue was obvious, and concern showed in Anya's eyes. Patiently, she waited and watched as he drank some water. He gathered himself, looked across the desk, and met her eyes as she watched him expectantly. With a sigh, he explained what had transpired, omitting nothing.

'I have moved on some nasty spirits in my time, but that was by far the most malicious,' he said with some feeling. 'The boy was no real problem to be honest. He was simply interested in the house, and was drawn by the activity and led astray by the other spirit. He was just moving things around and being annoying, thinking it was funny. He's gone now without much difficulty. He didn't give me any real problems, but he wouldn't answer my questions either, which was weird. The other spirit was a different matter altogether!'

The look of concern remained on her face as she replied. 'Do you have any idea where it came from?'

'I would have to tune in again to my guides for that.'

He closed his eyes, took a deep breath, and cleared his mind, calmly asking his guides for some answers. When the connection became strong, he answered.

'It appears it came from a relative, sent somehow from someone in your family on your grandfather's side. The spirit comes from someone who has been passed over for some time, someone of Indian origin, perhaps.'

Anya replied, 'Well, I don't get on with my family in India. They have always opposed me marrying my husband and moving from India to England. They are into all this sort of thing and sit in circles doing all kinds of dark energy manipulation.'

Mark sat quietly, closed his eyes again, and spoke silently to spirit.

'They sent it. It comes from them. Not specifically that spirit, but they wished you ill and this was the result. They envy your success. They are jealous of you moving to England, marrying a non-Hindu guy, and leaving the family in India.'

'Oh, they have always been angry with me ever since I married Robert. I don't even talk to my family now. Robert and I used to be quite affluent, but now everything seems to be going wrong. Business deals are falling through, and bills seem to be mounting up. It just seems we have had a spate of bad luck and misfortune.'

'That was the reason they sent it, because of jealousy and envy. They sent it to cause you problems and make your life difficult.' There was a thoughtful silence. 'It's gone now.'

'Can it come back?' she asked, with slight trepidation in her voice.

'No. It can't. I forced it back to its own realm with the help of my guides and Archangel Michael. I had to call in the big guns, and there is no way it's coming back. I can't stop them sending something else, but I have shielded the house. The shield won't last forever, but your house is clear. You should feel it immediately as you walk around, and you should notice a general lightness. I think things will improve for you now, but you'll have to put in some work yourself. Rewrite your own energy. The vibration you emit must be positive. You'll need to focus on things you do want in your life, rather than on what you don't. Then a change will start to occur and things should improve.'

'Is there anything I can do myself to prevent this happening again?'

'Well, you can cleanse your house regularly with sage, like I have. Also, you can sit in a central place, like your lounge, and meditate. Then imagine light coming down from the sky like a huge blanket descending or a shower of rain. Just imagine it covering your entire house, cleansing it and forming a protective bubble around the perimeter. That would be a good start. Any other problems, you can call me of course, and I am always willing to do a meditation with you.

'You have some power, but you need to learn discipline and control. And you lack knowledge. You could do with a good teacher, to be honest, if you wish to know more about these things. I sense you have been a bit of a loose cannon.' He smiled. 'In these situations, it's a bit like moths to a flame. Spirits and entities are attracted to a sensitive such as yourself. I can help you with all this if you want.'

'I suppose it would be a good idea for you to heal my family as well, just to cover all bases?'

'Yes, it would. We can do that later. Just give me a call when you are ready.'

Mark sensed it was time to leave, so he collected his things and walked with Anya to the front door.

'Thank you for what you have done today, Mark. I am so grateful.' Her huge smile was filled with warmth.

'You're welcome. If you have any problems, just give me a call or something and let me know.' He beamed back at her.

After he'd walked down the front path and through the gate, he glanced back at the house. That had been some experience. He'd known something interesting would come after meeting her that Friday night during Platform. That had turned out to be an understatement, and he wouldn't forget this one in a hurry, that's for sure. He climbed into his car and turned the ignition key, and the engine fired into life. Deep in thought, he eased the car away. Interesting indeed.

CHAPTER 6

THE WATCHERS

The three beings stood in the clouds, deep in conversation. They were beings of great power, beings of spirit realm, half in the earth plane and half in their own. They were pure energy in physical form. Almost.

One, called the Red Shaman, appeared Indian in nature and spoke first. He was clearly the leader of the three.

'*Interesting how he dealt with that.*'

'*He's passed the first grade with flying colours,*' Abatheer replied, another large powerful spirit being who glowed all white and was shaped in humanoid form.

The third being, called Malek, was smaller and also a glowing white humanoid. He interjected, '*Indeed. So what next, seeing as he is moving forward well? Perhaps it is time for the next stage?*'

'*Another test, you mean?*' Abatheer asked.

Both looked over to Red Shaman. Although slightly smaller in stature, he clearly had authority over the other two. No one knew his real name. Steeped in mystery, he was known only as Red Shaman and commanded huge respect—even from the supreme power above.

Red Shaman paused and steepled his fingers in front of his chest. A slight frown crossed his face, followed by a smirk.

'*Let's bring in some elementals. Some lesser demons should do the trick. This will test his ability to see through the layers.*'

Red Shaman sent out two beams of light from the centre of his hands to his fellow light beings. They morphed into two hideous gargoyles and leapt off the cloud and down to earth, both wailing with the shriek of banshees.

CHAPTER 7

MOTHS TO A FLAME

EMF [acronym]: Electromotive Force—EMF is generated by all electrical equipment. It is also generated by the neurology of all life forms. Spirit forces can influence it and be influenced by it.

Several months passed before Mark next heard from Anya. The leaves were well and truly down from the trees, and it looked like a hard winter was on its way. He had been busy during those last few months, but not only with work. Spirit had also granted him some time to get his house in order and to work on himself, honing both his skills and his environment. He didn't realise this was happening so that he would be refreshed and raring to go when the next stage was initiated. It was on a chilly November morning that he received a phone call from her.

'Hi, Mark. It's Anya.'

'Hi Anya. How are you? What's up?'

'It's the house again. There are things back in the house.'

'Really? What's going on then?'

He listened while she told him of recent events. As she brought him up to date, he realised there had been a fresh incursion in the household. More attacks had occurred. Anya felt concerned about her two teenage daughters. The younger of the two, Sarah, was 'sensitive' and had been seeing things in the house, making her feel uncomfortable and distressed, which was most unlike her. She had become more 'aware' and 'sensitive' to spiritual activity as she got older. Anya was worried, so she wanted Mark to see them both and check that everything was okay.

She didn't go into too much further detail over the phone, and he decided it was better to leave it until he arrived. When he was there he would be able to get the rest of the information he needed. No amount of talking on the phone could replace being in the house itself. They agreed that he should visit a few days later, and so it was that Mark found himself, one cool morning, again driving to her house. A little frost had formed during the night, but it had thawed in the sunshine, leaving the roads damp. Not knowing exactly what to expect, Mark had made the usual mental preparations for protection and guidance prior to his arrival.

He felt somewhat apprehensive as he knocked on the front door, and he was a little relieved to be greeted by Anya with a beaming smile.

'Hello, Mark. How are you? Come in, come in.'

Mark stepped through the doorway onto the brown carpet, removed his shoes at the front door, and left them outside out of politeness. Anya led him into the study, where he hung up his coat and placed his belongings on the desk. His first impression was that the house felt neutral, but a full examination would have to be done before he could make a complete assessment.

Anya pulled a chair from under the table, which served as her desk, and started talking.

'Mark, I want you to check out a room later. It's Sarah's room. She isn't staying in it at the moment but is sleeping with me. She says she doesn't feel comfortable in there, and she seems to be quite agitated at the moment. She's very spiritual, you know, and sensitive, and I'm concerned about her. She's not sleeping, and she's complaining of headaches and being on edge. It's very strange, not like her at all.'

He nodded. 'Okay, I'll have a look at her too.'

'The strangest thing happened. I was in the lounge one night with Robert, sitting on the sofa. You know the one? The TV was on, and suddenly we heard this massive bang behind us, like something heavy dropping on the floor. Robert heard it too, and we both jumped. We checked behind the sofa, but there was nothing there or even close. We looked everywhere and could find nothing fallen over. And another night we were watching TV, and all the electrics for the TV system went off. Nothing else did—just the TV, the DVD, and the Sky box. We couldn't watch TV for an hour. We checked the sockets, plugs, everything. Then, suddenly, it just all came back on! There has been lots of weird stuff going on with the electrics in the house. So we called an electrician, and he came round but could find nothing wrong with our wiring or the TV. I'm telling you, Mark, something is going on round here.'

'Hmm,' he said thoughtfully. 'It does sound like it, doesn't it?' He paused for a few seconds. 'Let's go upstairs and have a look where you want me to do the healing. You said you had a treatment couch already set up, didn't you?'

'Yes, it's in Sarah's room. It's the biggest and gives you the most room to work.'

They walked silently on the soft brown carpet that covered all the floors in the house and ascended the stairs. Once they reached the main landing, they entered Sarah's room. Mark looked around and picked up on something in the corner—a presence. He focused his attention and saw that it was a female spirit, an earthbound, which didn't seem to be malicious in anyway. Not wishing to worry Anya unduly by mentioning it, he asked her to leave and allow him to set up the energies for healing. He would deal with the spirit then.

Mark turned his back to the door and allowed Anya to walk out. Then he focused his attention again on the spirit in the corner. He pulled down his protective bubble and closed his chakras, and then he called his guides in closer, drawing from their strength. He prepared himself to move the spirit on, and spoke to her in his mind.

'It's time for you to move on. What are you doing here?'

'I don't know,' the voice replied in his mind. 'I'm just here. I'm not sure why.'

'Well, it's time for you to move on. Let me help you. Will you leave?'

There was a pause, and then the spirit whispered a quiet yes in reply.

She was only hanging around due to the spiritual activity in the house. This often happens. Spirits can pick up on other spiritual activity and be attracted to it. Mark called down a golden gateway, and a circle of light appeared in the room, with a small golden stairway just below it that led directly up to the entrance. He encouraged the spirit to move on with soft words and gestures, and he watched her walk steadily up the glowing light staircase towards the waiting gateway. When she stepped through and disappeared, a sense of peace emanated from the glowing light, and seconds later the gateway winked out.

Mark felt about to make sure she hadn't left any negative residue. Then he set up the energies in the room to prepare for healing Anya's two daughters. It's important to have a positively energised room in which to heal or to do any spiritual work.

Two hours later, he had completed the healing of both girls. He called Anya up and gestured for her to take a seat.

'They were both fine, nothing to worry about. However, there was a female spirit in this room whom I moved on with no problem. It may have been making Sarah feel uncomfortable, but she wasn't causing any problems. I think she was just here out of interest to see what was going on, drawn by the activity here. Anyway, she's gone now.'

Anya sighed. The slightly alarmed look she had adopted when he mentioned the female spirit disappeared to be replaced by a neutral expression.

'Mark, can you check out the back room for me? It feels very strange, and I'm sure something is in there.'

He stood and nodded towards the door. 'Okay, show me which room.'

Anya led him into a double bedroom on the other side of the house.

CHAPTER 8

INTERFERENCE

Demon [noun]: A set of negative thought forms that has coalesced into a discarnate or body-less entity.

When Mark stepped inside the bedroom, he could see it was full of electronic equipment. On the right was a long table with two laptops, an assortment of CDs, and some musical equipment. A desk sat opposite the doorway, next to a double bed flanked by two bedside cabinets. Underneath the window, which faced the front garden, was a storage unit with a portable music centre and even more CDs. Two electric alarm clocks also ticked away, along with phone chargers and a mass of electric cables and sockets strewn about, particularly under the table.

A layer of dust covered the equipment, as well as the tables and an old rocking horse, which sat motionless amongst a pile of boxes. Though it was a relatively large and spacious room, it had an oppressive feel to it and a confusing energy. Mark picked up a buzzing feeling caused by the EMF from the electronic equipment. He could hear a slight humming.

'It won't be pleasant to sleep in here. It will send the brain into apoplexy and mess with the flow of your meridians,' he said.

The electronic equipment was the obvious cause of bad energy. 'Is the equipment ever switched off?'

'No,' she replied.

'Mm, you could do with some mains suppression filters for the equipment, and a few crystals to absorb the stray energies.'

Mark felt uneasy. He looked up in an attempt to get to the bottom of this uncomfortable feeling. He couldn't say why. It was just a bump-on-the-back-of-the-neck sensation.

As he stared straight at the far corner of the ceiling by the window, he saw a small dark figure. It crouched like Spiderman, pressing itself right into the recess, clinging there with feet and hands facing back, sticking to the walls. It was a minor demon.

The obvious source of the energy disturbance (the electronic equipment) had made him miss the entity entirely. Now it was doing its best to remain anonymous by hiding in the corner. Piercing yellow eyes stared balefully at him. Mark pointed to the corner and spoke sharply to Anya.

'You need to leave the room now. There is something in here I have to deal with.'

She heard the urgency in his voice, and with a fearful glance at the corner indicated, she turned and left the room with haste, closing the door behind her.

Once he heard the door close, Mark brought his attention to bear on this entity and looked at it carefully. Small but menacing, it continued to stare straight back at him. It was silent and intense, and its yellow eyes locked with his from within a vague black surround that was clearly its head. The body and limbs were black. It was the size of a small monkey, but it bore no resemblance to any earthbound primate. Its outer edge was vaguely indistinct, slightly blurred. Both its arms and legs were pressed back into the recess, holding its position.

Mark glanced around and saw that there were two other demons situated strategically in adjacent corners of the ceiling. They were motionless, malevolent in their silence, like slow poison seeping into the room. Their looks and position were almost identical to each other. He gathered his strength, and energy shot out of his hands, wrapping around the main demon he'd seen first, pinning it in the corner before it could react. The demon gauged the strength of its new bonds. It was slightly bigger than the others, and Mark sensed it was sentient. It could both think and talk.

'*What are you doing here?*'

Silence greeted his question. He tightened the now encircling bonds and waited for a reply. Long seconds passed, but silence was still the answer, accompanied by a stare of increasing intensity and defiance. This was a battle of wills. Mark squeezed further and watched, testing and waiting.

'*I can do this all day if you want.*'

He gave an extra surge of power. A minute passed, then two. Still silence. It was Mark's will against the demon's. Then the demon slumped visibly. Intimidated into submission, the demon sagged a little and capitulated. Mark tried the question again.

'*What are you doing here?*'

'*I was sent here.*' The answer rasped in Mark's mind.

'*By whom?*'

'*By my family.*'

'*Why?*'

'*Because we were told to.*'

'*Who told you to?*'

'*I don't know.*' Resentment filled its voice.

With a slight squeeze of its bonds, Mark repeated the question. '*Who told you to?*'

The demon gave a grudging look. '*We owed them.*'

Mark received a sense that the demons' hierarchy had ordered them to come here, as they owed a debt to another family. They were fulfilling that debt by being here. Their task: to spread negativity and chaos. Then he made the connection. The family was Anya's family! Although this one was only a minor worker demon, it was in charge of the others and the only one that was sentient.

He had obtained all the information that he was likely to get from it, so he called his dark guides closer. Two of them stepped forward and positioned themselves each side of the demon. Working in harmony with them and just by thinking of it, a dark portal was summoned. Circular and black in colour, a few feet in diameter and almost opaque, it appeared just above head height on the wall in front of him. They brought it forth to send the demon back where it came from. His dark helpers held it from each side and guided it towards the portal, with Mark's light bonds still securing it, and pushed it through with a minimum of resistance.

Then Mark turned his attention to the minor mindless demons. He looked in each corner to study them for a few seconds. They were not intelligent; their task was just to send out negative energy and upset the balance of the house, forming a dark energy grid in the room.

Mark pushed out tendrils of energy and secured each demon in its respective corner, while his dark guides went to the first one and formed a new portal in front of it. With Mark securing and pushing lightly, the dark guides escorted it into their own realm. The process was repeated with a new portal formed each time.

Mark glanced around the room to make sure they were all gone. Then he summoned light up from the earth, and it rose from the ground upwards, pressing tightly against the walls of the room, rising to the ceiling and filling the corners, where only moments before dark entities had inhabited, radiating their poisonous energy.

He moved to each corner, and light shone from his hands to blast away the dark residue, bringing light where darkness had been so that it would not return. Then he stood in the centre of the room and drew up more light from the earth, focused on cleansing, bringing in stillness and peace. For two minutes he stood thus, channelling, clearing, and burning away any remnants. When he had finished, he dropped his hands and surveyed his handiwork. With a nod of satisfaction he left the room and walked downstairs to speak to Anya. No doubt she was burning to know what was going on.

She was in the kitchen, fussing around the work surface, keeping herself busy. A cup of steaming Chinese herbal tea sat on the table, with a second empty cup next to the recently boiled kettle. When he told her what had happened, a look of mild alarm crossed her delicate features.

'Let's go upstairs and see how you feel,' he said when he had finished his narrative. He stood up and turned to walk upstairs, knowing that she would follow.

On the landing at the top of the stairs, he paused and looked up at the ceiling for a second. Something was niggling him. He decided to let it pass and spoke to Anya.

'See how you feel in here.'

They entered Sarah's room and he moved aside, beckoned Anya, and asked her how it felt now.

For a couple of seconds she scanned the room, looking about. Then she turned back and nodded. 'Yes, it feels much better.'

'Well, it's clear and safe now, but I need to come back tomorrow to finish the job. I'm too tired at the moment, and it needs my full attention. It will be fine for tonight.'

With that Mark walked downstairs and, after a brief goodbye, left the house and climbed into his car.

Back at home, he sat down gratefully to eat a late lunch of grilled cod, rice, and fresh vegetables, lightly steamed. As he ate, he ruminated on what was happening with Anya and her house. Something deeper was going on here, and he hadn't got to the bottom of it yet.

What was going on? What was that feeling he got from above on the landing?

He pondered for a minute and then let it go and relaxed. When he'd finished his food, he moved over to the cream leather sofa and lay down for a nap. He'd get to the bottom of it tomorrow morning.

CHAPTER 9

RAISING THE BAR

Red Shaman and the two other powerful light beings reconvened in the clouds.

'*His training is moving ahead well,*' Abatheer reported.

'*Yes, he performed adequately,*' said Malek. '*Perhaps it is time to raise the bar? Give him a real test? What do you think?*'

Red Shaman steepled his fingers again. The two light beings exchanged knowing glances. Both recognised the familiar gesture. They turned back to their superior and waited expectantly.

'*I liked the way he dealt with those lesser demons we sent him—the way he sensed them and then showed appropriate force—and insight in questioning too. Perhaps something more challenging would be good now.*'

'*And what shall we offer him now to learn from?*' Abatheer asked.

Red Shaman replied. '*Let's send in a full-fledged demon. Something from myth.*'

Abatheer and Malek exchanged worried glances.

'*Are you sure he is ready for that?*' Malek asked.

'*There is only one way to find out. Let's send the hound in.*'

At this point Red Shaman changed both colour and shape. He was not a pretty sight in the first place. As a werewolf, he was positively grotesque and even more imposing.

'*This will separate the wheat from the chaff,*' he snarled as he bounded off.

CHAPTER 10

GHOST GAMES

Guides [noun]: These are discarnate aspects of our consciousness and being. They are sometimes ascended masters, angels or even archangels. Some think they are even future versions of ourselves. They look after us, protect us and point us in the right direction. They never sleep and love us unconditionally. Many people live their whole lives unaware of their presence.

The next morning Mark made his way to Anya's house again and knocked on the door at 10 a.m. sharp.

'Come on in, Mark. It's good to see you,' she said, ushering him into her lounge.

As usual, he took off his shoes and left them outside on the door mat before following her in.

'How did you sleep last night?' he asked.

'Better, thanks. The bedrooms definitely felt better than they were. Sarah slept in her own room last night.'

'Good. Well, let me have a look around the house, and I'll see what's going on.'

With that, he looked around the lounge and focused his attention, looking in the corners and along the walls and feeling the energy about him. He didn't have to walk to each corner unless there was something very specific to investigate, like behind a TV.

Within a few seconds he saw demons identical to the ones he'd detected yesterday, perched in each ceiling corner of the lounge like dark parasites, seeping their poison into the room. He sensed they were non-intelligent servants of a greater force. He reinforced his protective shield of energy about him and called down more light from above. He called his guides in closer, but they were way ahead of him. His team of spirit workers were already spreading around the house like light sentinels, strategically placing themselves in key locations.

Positioned in the centre of the room, he called down a dark portal to each corner in turn and extended white beams of light from his hands. The light wrapped around the first demon, and it was pulled out of the corner towards the waiting portal. Dark guides moved forward, positioning themselves on either side to walk it through into the waiting blackness, where it disappeared into the realm it belonged to. Three more times he repeated the exercise, and the portals winked out when he was finished. Next he called up a deep purple light from the earth, and it permeated through the floor and entered the room, stretching from wall to wall. It left no gaps as it rose to the ceiling and cleansed and burnt away the negative residue.

With a nod of satisfaction, Mark walked into the hallway and through to Anya's study, looking around vigilantly. Similar non-sentient minor demons inhabited each corner of the room here too. With a slight frown he went into the utility room across the hall and checked there as well. Sure enough, in each ceiling corner it was the same. He had a feeling it would be like that throughout the house. Repeating the process he'd used in the lounge and preparing mentally to do upstairs afterwards, he removed the parasitical demons and cleansed each room with purple light from the earth.

Satisfied, he called out to Anya that he was going upstairs.

'Okay,' she replied, 'I'll stay down here.'

At the top of the stairs Mark paused for a second, getting his bearings and extending his senses. He knew where he had to go first, and he strode the few paces necessary to reach the bedroom to the right, across the landing where he had been yesterday. He walked over, entered, and noticed an interesting phenomenon. In each ceiling corner a small dark mass had coalesced, no more than four to six inches across. It appeared a new demon was forming in each corner here too, the same as the ones he had already removed. Strange, he thought. He had cleared the room only yesterday and they were reforming already.

No, they were not reforming, he realised. New ones were birthing. He learned several things immediately. First, something must be working actively behind these minor-level demons to summon more of them so quickly. Second, the whole house needed to be shielded. Third, and more importantly, the source had to be closed, whatever it was. None of these things had he done yet.

He raised his hands and blasted light out into the corners, burning away the dark energy before it could coalesce and densify. It was short work to finish that room, and he moved into the others, one by one. He found the same demons in every corner, and they swiftly followed suit, nullified and removed—right until he entered Sarah's room. At that point something completely unexpected happened.

Mark was sitting in the centre, seated on a swivel desk chair. He closed his eyes and concentrated. He sent his awareness about the room, checking each ceiling corner, and realised that in here the small parasitical entities were not present. He reasoned that this was because of the healing work he had done previously. The positive healing energy in here would have made things considerably more difficult for anything negative to be in the room. He initiated a more focused state to finish cleansing and entered a deeper state of stillness, deepening his breathing, becoming more relaxed, and completely focusing on the room and the energy.

In the background, outside Sarah's room, he heard paper rustling, as though someone was shuffling papers around on a desk, tidying up. As far as he was aware, no one was upstairs, and he frowned slightly. Must have been mistaken about where it was coming from, he mused. At first he thought it was probably Anya in the study downstairs. The rustling continued on and off for a few minutes, and he grew certain it was coming from upstairs. But his mind told him Anya was downstairs and the only one in the house, so it couldn't be. He was somewhat perplexed, but he thought his mind must be distorting things while he was in a semi-meditative state.

He resumed his positive stillness, but his reverie was broken moments later when he heard footsteps as clear as day, walking across the landing from the stairs to the office bedroom. This was surprising. He hadn't heard anyone walking up the stairs. Even though he was in a semi-meditative state, he worked to maintain an active awareness of his surroundings. This was crucial to doing the job.

But still someone was definitely walking around up here. He carried on with the clearing but also kept a careful ear on what was happening upstairs as the footsteps continued. Every now and then they would cross the landing and then return to the office bedroom again, where they would walk about inside.

About a minute or so before he finished cleansing the room, the footsteps stopped, and he heard nothing more. A search of the upstairs confirmed that no one was up there. Again, he had heard no one go downstairs. Mark walked down to the lounge and found Anya in the kitchen preparing her usual Columbian coffee.

'Hi, I'm done. Do you want to come up and check the rooms? See how they feel to you?' he asked.

She put down her coffee and followed him back upstairs and into Sarah's bedroom.

'Have you been up here at all?'

'No, I have been downstairs all the time. Why?'

'I heard someone moving around in that spare room over there, papers rustling and things. Heard someone walking across the landing too. You say you haven't been up here?'

'No, not once'

'And no one else is in?'

'No.'

He paused for a second, and a tense smile crossed his features. Something was playing with him and was still here in the house.

'Then someone is having a laugh at our expense.'

He sensed something above him again and glanced up. Watching. Gauging. And it didn't feel nice.

CHAPTER 11

THE LOFT

Archangel [noun]: A highly evolved and ancient consciousness who marshals angels and ascended masters and acts as a direct conduit to the godhead. Archangels rarely incarnate fully on the earth plane other than as an energy.

'What's in the loft, Anya?'

'Just boxes and bits and pieces. The usual stuff you have up there. 'Why'?

Mark paused before he answered. He frowned, 'I'm not sure exactly. Something doesn't feel right.'

When he looked up at the loft hatch and felt what was going on above, he heard a voice, deep and piercing in his mind. He knew immediately it was coming from above, laughing and mocking him.

'You think you have cleared this house and rid it of us?' More mocking laughter peeled out. *'You have failed. We are still here!'*

Surprised, but not wanting to alarm Anya and let on what he had heard, he turned towards her and said in as much of a neutral tone as he could muster, 'I need to get into the loft if possible to check it out. Is that okay?'

'Sure. Let me just get the tool we use to open it.'

Seconds later she reappeared with a slender stick a few feet long and proceeded to release the hatch door. It swung down silently, and once the hatch had settled, Mark looked into the opening as she reached up and pulled down the extending ladder to the landing floor.

'Okay,' he said. 'You can leave it with me now.'

Anya left him, and he climbed the stairs and pushed his head through into the loft area. Dark and cold, it provided a stark contrast to the rest of the house below. He stepped up fully and climbed into the loft. As he stood up he experienced a sense of trepidation. There was little room to move. Boxes were stacked all around from floor to ceiling, extending right under the rafters. Peering into its inky depths, he could see very little. The bulk of the loft was shrouded in darkness. A quick search revealed a light switch, which he flicked on. A bare bulb hanging from one of the rafters flared into life, providing rudimentary light and a great deal of shadows and dark places, full of foreboding. With the light now on, more questions than answers were raised as to what may be up here.

He stood motionless and sensed a stillness—an unnatural stillness—and shivered. Large wisps of condensation blew out of his mouth as he exhaled. It was freezing up here! Un-insulated lofts can be cold, but this was very different.

A central path, free of boxes, ran either side of the loft hatch, and Mark had to step over the opening to traverse it. He walked around as much as he could. Then he stood on one side of the hatch and held out his hands, waist height and palms up, calling down light to start cleansing the area and getting a better feel for what was going on up here.

When he faced the far end of the loft, he felt something more, something darker, in front of him. He stepped forward as far as he could go, and there were more boxes stacked up at different heights. The dim light bulb behind did him little to illuminate the large spaces behind these stacked boxes. Anything could be hiding there.

Shadows formed wherever he looked. He could see nothing, but he certainly sensed something. It was almost tangible, but he couldn't quite locate it. He paused and gathered his attention and then felt outwards, sending feelers behind the boxes into the dark places where he couldn't see.

Then he felt it. A definite presence. Hidden in the shadows, dark and malevolent, but trying to remain undetected. Mark moved closer and peered into the gloom on his left. He slowly got a feel for what was there, drawing it out and shining energetic light to peel back the layers of shadow.

Moments later a silhouette appeared, skulking behind some of the boxes under a rafter. It was large and black, resembling a massive dog or wolf. Realising it had been discovered, it stepped out from behind the rafter, growling with menace. It was huge.

Like a werewolf from stories of old, it came on all fours further out in the open, but still in the shadows. Short jet-black fur provided a stark contrast to the yellow slitted eyes that locked onto his own just feet away. The head was enormous, with gaping jaws showing huge canine teeth as it snarled its anger. The hairs stood up on the nape of Mark's neck as he gave an involuntary shiver. Shields dropped down instantly around him. His guides' hackles stood up as they moved forward with incredible speed. He could feel their energies overlapping his. This was not some minor underling like the others.

He raised his hands without hesitation and gathered power. Light shot out from his upraised palms, streaming towards the demon and wrapping around its body. Long cables of power entwined its limbs and head. The demon growled and laughed scornfully.

'You can't hold me, human.'

Mark intensified the energy stream from his hands and held it fast, but he knew he didn't have much time.

'*Your time is done here. You're no longer required and will go back to your own realm,*' he proclaimed with force.

Then he called down a dark portal to transport it back to its demonic realm, and, gathering his strength, he began to pull it towards the black opening to the underworld. He had to force yet more power out of his hands and tighten the bonds surrounding it. Slowly the demon moved towards the portal. Mark's guides, like two huge dark bodyguards, supported him, lending their strength, pushing and pulling. The seconds dragged by, and movement was slow.

Minutes later the beast was still not through the portal. Mark realised he needed help. Mentally calling out loud for Archangel Michael, he strained to keep the momentum going. Beads of sweat stood out on his brow with the effort. Seconds later, Archangel Michael appeared in front of him, hovering a few inches above the floor. Surrounded in Michael's light blue nimbus, Mark immediately felt strength flow around him and throughout the whole vicinity. The archangel supplied the vital power he so desperately needed. With renewed and enhanced vigour, together they drew the demon forwards.

The werewolf went berserk. Leaning back on its mighty haunches, its talons gouged the floor while it twisted and turned every which way, struggling to break its bonds and escape its imminent demise from the looming dark portal. Muscles bulged under its black coated flanks, and it snapped and snarled as it fought with every ounce of its strength, resisting every millimetre with extreme prejudice.

Inexorably it slipped the last few inches to the edge of the portal, until it finally tipped inside with a scream of rage and disappeared into the abyss, back into its own realm. The dark portal winked shut almost immediately, leaving no trace of its existence.

Seconds later Archangel Michael vanished, and Mark stood alone with his guides. He took a few deep breaths and surveyed the area, feeling for the demon, checking it really was gone. With a huge sigh of relief, he called down light again, arms raised to just below chest height, asking all his spiritual helpers to aid him and bathe the entire area.

As the energy changed within, searing away any dark residue left behind, he felt the power burn within him as the light shone out all around, permeating every molecule in the vicinity. It spread from the loft, and then throughout the house, down and down, extending to the gardens and surrounding land, to the outer edges of the plot. No corner was left unlit, no object left untouched. All the negative energy was burned away, peeling back any darkness that was left. The brightness rose up in intensity and continued for a few seconds more. And then it was done.

With arms dropping to his side, Mark opened his eyes and looked around. It was clear. He then moved to the hatch, flicked off the light switch, and climbed down the ladder to the landing. For a moment or two he planted his feet on the floor and sent out his spirit eyes, feeling the movement of the house and the vibration within. It pulsated with positive energy. He breathed a steady sigh. It was over.

'Has the curse finally ended with the removal of that last demon?' Mark asked the heavens.

His guides answered his silent question in the affirmative. Mark drew up the ladder and secured the loft hatch. Then he walked downstairs to speak to Anya to let her know what had happened.

'Will I tell her everything?' he asked himself. She deserved to know and would understand. The decision was made swiftly. He would tell her almost everything, but he would play it down so she wasn't too alarmed. She didn't need to know all the details of how deep and dark this had really gone. It would serve no purpose other than upset her and cause bad memories.

'No,' he thought. 'It's better she doesn't know everything."

With this decision made, he walked into Anya's study and told her what he had witnessed. A little later he said his goodbyes to a stunned but grateful Anya and left the house.

He glanced back as he walked down the front garden path and wondered if he would be called there again. One thing he knew for sure was that it wouldn't be the last he would see of Anya and her family. Mark climbed into his car and muttered a silent prayer that their next encounter would occur under better circumstances, and then he started his drive home.

CHAPTER 12

POSSESSION

'*That pushed him,*' Malek said.

'*He did well, considering what he had to deal with,*' Abatheer said.

'*Not bad at all,*' Red Shaman replied. '*His progress is uniform and only what we would expect. He continues to move in the right direction. Perhaps there is hope for him to fulfil his role yet. Let's throw in a few anomalies. I feel a real lesson is in order.*'

He gave directions to both light beings.

'*Contact the Archangels and seek permission for the next stage of his learning. He needs to know new things. A lesson in power is required, lest he feels the dark owns all.*'

'*They may not like us asking this of them,*' Abatheer protested.

'*They'll help us when they are aware of the full picture. They are not the only ones who have connections. Some things outweigh even the Archangels' authority. Tell them we want to bring in a few complications and see how he deals with entities that have latched onto people.*'

Red Shaman and the two light beings stepped closer together and held hands in a triangle. Red Shaman incanted in a language not heard for over a million years. The cloud beneath them darkened, and an upwelling of dark clogging energy came up through their feet and entered their hearts.

The hearts of the three light beings turned black and merged into one, floating in the space between them. Seconds later the hearts separated, entering each light being, who reacted as though struck.

Red Shaman issued another unrecognisable curse, and all three morphed into dark witch doctors of unknown origin and plummeted down to the Earth Plane.

Mark would have little idea what was coming his way.

CHAPTER 13

A CHANCE MEETING

Serendipity [noun]: An event which looks like a mere stroke of luck to those on the Earth Plane but is actually an orchestrated encounter by entities from higher planes.

A couple of months later, Mark took a trip to the local town centre to browse in the large bookstore for some books in the Mind, Body, and Spirit section. The woman who was running a course he was on at the time had recommended a book about Carl Jung that she felt would be an interesting read for him.

He took the time to wander around, but after a while, unable to find what he wanted, he asked the girl behind the desk. She was a pretty girl of about nineteen. After listening to his enquiry, she walked him to the relevant section. They both had a good look around, but their search for the book proved fruitless despite their combined efforts. After ten minutes or so of hunting around, Mark thanked her and said he would carry on looking himself.

He turned on his heels to continue browsing and spotted Anya sitting and reading in one of the few light tan armchairs several feet away from him. She was wearing a blue patterned blouse and skirt and brown boots. Her coat was thrown over her lap, and she was engrossed in her book and hadn't seen him.

He approached her with a big smile, and she suddenly looked up and rewarded him with a smile of her own in return. She seemed genuinely pleased to see him.

'Sit down,' she said warmly, pointing to the chair next to her. 'What are you doing here?'

'I'm just looking for a book that's been recommended to me. How are you?'

'Okay,' she replied. She gave him another big smile and pointed across the shop floor. 'Why don't we get a coffee in Howden's coffee shop just over there?'

'Sure. 'Why not?'

She closed her book, gathered her belongings, and they walked over. Anya gestured to a table and chairs in the corner. 'Let's sit over there,' she said. 'I've been meaning to talk to you. So much has happened. What do you want to drink?'

'Peppermint tea, please.'

She placed her things down on the table and crossed over to the counter, where she stood in the short queue to order their drinks. Mark took his coat off and sat down. A few minutes later, Anya returned with steaming cups of tea and coffee.

'So,' he asked, taking a sip of tea, 'what's been happening?'

'You know I kept saying something was wrong with the house? Well, it's come back again. I couldn't even sit in the lounge on that sofa, and I didn't want to be left alone. I was sure something had come back. I was going to call you, but I knew you were abroad, so I had to find someone else. I looked on the Internet and found this website online with people who did similar things to you. You know I trust my instincts, so I rang them and arranged for the man to come round and look at the house. I was convinced there was something there again.'

'What was the name of the website and the guy who came?' Mark recognised the names of both the man and the site. 'I know this person. He is very good at what he does. You did the right thing. What did he have to say?'

'He had a good look around and found some other things. Apparently, my house is above an old graveyard from many centuries ago, and there is a dark hole under my sofa which holds many restless spirits.'

'That will be a gateway, so to speak.'

'Yes, and he said that there is a local priest who is controlling this gateway. During the day he is a clergyman at a local church, but at night he is into all kinds of dark stuff. It is this priest who is allowing the evil spirits to enter my house. I told him about the Hindu chanting CDs I had been playing, and he said I needed to continue doing that and keep lights on around the sofa area. He went around the house and found loads more things in different places, particularly my study, which I couldn't even go into any more. I tell you, Mark, I couldn't even walk through the door—it was so horrible. Anyway, he got rid of everything in the house and then did whatever he did to the gateway—closed it, I think—and he also got rid of the priest's control of the gateway.'

'How is it now?' He leaned forward and concentrated more.

'All seems fine now, much better, and I can go in the study too.'

'Good, I'm glad. While I had dealt with your family curse, he was obviously meant to come in and deal with this while I was away. He's very good at what he does, and you made the right choice. It's important to remember we all have our talents and specialities, much like any other profession. Some mediums can see auras, and some see spirits. Some hear them, some sense them, some feel them, and some just seem to know what is going on.'

'I see,' Anya replied. After a moment she continued thoughtfully. 'I want you to do some healing on myself and Robert. I have been thinking about you the last couple of days, and—funny—now I bump into you. I've been meaning to call you for a while, but one thing after another came up, and, well, you're here now. Robert has something in him, I'm sure. He has been unbearable for the last week, and I know he needs to see you.

I have been trying to talk him into it. Also, I know that there is something still in me.'

Even looking at her carefully, Mark could see nothing obvious.

'I can't see anything in you at the moment, but I would need to tune in to you in a proper session.'

Anya's phone rang. 'Hi, darling, how are you? I'm just in Howden's with Mark. Why don't you come and join us?' She put the phone down. 'Robert is just in town, so he's coming over to join us.'

'Cool.'

They occupied themselves with general light-hearted chat for about ten minutes until Robert arrived. Robert was a short, heavily built man, a few inches over five foot, with brown hair and a tanned complexion. He wore cream trousers, black shoes, and a dark blue coat, and he smiled with genuine warmth.

'Hi, Robert, good to see you. How are you?' Mark greeted him as he strolled over to their table.

'I'm good, thanks.' Robert smiled back. He sensed something was not so good though.

Anya got up and ordered them all another drink, and Mark glanced around Howden's. It was busy, and most of the tables were occupied. They were in their own little corner, kept empty because of the noise from the food refrigeration unit next to them. There were still tables nearby though, and the low chatter of many voices filled the large open space. However, each group of people appeared to be in their own little world though.

Anya returned with the drinks and sat down. As they chatted over the next few minutes, Mark noticed something about Robert. That awareness of his, when he knew something was there, had suddenly come to life. He looked intently around Robert's body, and then directly at him. As Mark's vision adjusted, he saw something dark encircling Robert's energy field.

Mark tuned in, feeling Robert's aura and the surrounding energy. It wasn't good, and he got a feeling of unease. Something was very wrong, and his body switched to high alert. His guides stepped in closer, making their presence known. The two main guides loomed either side of him like sentinels.

This was the final confirmation that something was up and that he needed to resolve it there and then.

CHAPTER 14

THE COFFEE SHOP

Aura [noun]: Every living being generates an etheric or auric field, and at the same time the physical body is crystallised and maintained by this same field. The aura mirrors the emotional state and health of the living organism. The organism receives its essential life force, or chi, from the auric field, which in turn receives it from the surrounding universe. One cannot exist without the other.

With another look around, Mark considered their location again and acknowledged where they were. This was a busy coffee bar in a bustling town centre. His sense of unease rose steadily. Now he knew something needed to be done, and he couldn't ignore it even if he wanted to.

Barely aware of the conversation between Anya and Robert, he interrupted and looked seriously at Robert.

'Robert, you have something on you, and I can't just leave it. Can I take it off you?'

He hesitated only briefly. 'Yes, sure.'

'I know we are in the middle of Howden's, and it's not an ideal location, but I have to do it.'

Mark sat on the chair next to Robert and closed his eyes. Then he spoke to his guides directly, asking for help, guidance, and permission to do what was needed. When they stepped in closer, he felt their presence grow stronger, offering the support he needed. He gathered concentration and focused his thoughts, sending his roots down deep into the earth from his feet. This would bypass all the surface energy, where hundreds of people— potentially thousands—tread every week, leaving their energetic detritus for all to pick up. He needed to go deep, right to the core of Mother Earth. He would need to tap into her vital energy in its purest form to support and protect them all. Once he'd summoned up energetic light from below through his roots, he felt the tingling as it entered his feet and travelled upwards. His whole body felt alive and buzzing as he filled himself with beautiful empowering energy.

When he felt white light come down from above, Mark encased himself in a protective bubble and then expanded it to encircle the three of them and the immediate vicinity. A glance over at Robert revealed a malevolence emanating, which was coming not from him but from somewhere else. His guides stepped yet closer on either side of him, a sure sign of work to be done.

Acutely aware of their surroundings and his guides' close proximity, he paused to think. *'What about where we are? All these people? Surely they will notice?'*

'Do not be concerned,' they answered, and a feeling that everything would be okay came through. *'Trust … trust.'*

He turned his attention back to Robert and saw something attached to his heart centre. That was where the root of this entity was, at his core. Mark opened his awareness and received the feeling it was a grandfather vibration from Robert's father's side.

The entity didn't want to be seen and was deliberately hiding itself, limiting how much was exposed. Spirits can do that if they know how. Existing as energy, unencumbered by physical material form like us, they can hide and change their form to fool you. But still Mark could feel and see it, with his guides filling in the blanks, so there was no escape. This was an unfriendly relative, and it most certainly did not want Mark here. It sensed what he was about to do and the very obvious threat he represented.

A sense of anger washed over Mark from the entity as it cried, *'Leave me alone. I am here to help him!'*

Mark steeled himself and asked Robert to lean forward. He placed one hand behind his back, a few inches from touching. His right hand hovered over Robert's chest and heart space. He directed energy out from his palms and held the energies around Robert's heart in a vice-like grip, increasing the power until he was satisfied he was fully in control. Once he felt that the spirit was secure, he looked at Robert.

'I am picking up that it's your grandfather from your father's side. Is he in spirit?'

'Yes, why? Is it him?'

Mark looked intently at Robert. 'Was he a nice man?'

'No, he wasn't. He very much thought men should be men and women should be at home in the kitchen doing women's jobs. I don't think he had any respect for women, and he was like that for as long as I remember.'

'Okay, I think it's him with you now. He is holding you back and is attached to your heart centre. He believes he is helping you. He wants to keep you the way he was—the way other men of your ancestral line were. He doesn't like you breaking the mould. He actually thinks he's helping you. Just give me a minute.'

Mark focused again on his hold around this spirit that was embedded in Robert's heart space and glanced around the room. Despite the position he was in with Robert—leaning towards him, for all intents and purposes to the casual observer having his arms around him in a hug—not one single person was looking at them. The coffee house was full, not a chair was empty, and yet not a single eye was turned their way. The other customers were, thankfully, totally oblivious to what was going on. It was as though they weren't even there. Mark could barely hear the cacophony of conversation from all these people as he removed the last vestiges of his surroundings from his consciousness.

He contacted the spirit directly once more. *'You're no longer wanted. You need to move on.'*

'No,' it roared back.

Mark called down two portals, one of light and one of dark, and a bright circle of gold light appeared as a disc about five feet away just to the side above Robert's head. Mark couldn't see through it, but he had an awareness of considerable depth beyond the entrance. An equivalent yet opposite dark portal opened alongside it. It was jet black and opaque with the same sense of depth behind it. The golden portal was the entrance to the first level of spirit. The dark one went straight to the underworld's first level, which is really something you would wish to avoid. Only the worst cases go there if they're not evolved enough to move into the light yet.

'You have a choice,' Mark said, using his spirit voice. *'You can leave voluntarily and move on, or you can be moved by me regardless.'*

He paused, allowing his words to sink in. This ancestor, one of Robert's grandfathers, now had a decision to make. If it made the higher choice, it could step into the light. Alternatively, if it was not ready to move on and make that shift in energy, another destination was on offer. The decision of which portal to take, was its own to make.

Mark waited, but not for long. You can't hang around with dark spirits. You have to take control or else you will lose said control and they may escape—or worse, escape and cause more harm elsewhere.

He waited for a few seconds more. Then he took a deep breath and gathered himself. The spirit wasn't moving, so he directed energy through his hands and, with a twisting motion, took hold of its essence and with a huge surge ripped it out of the heart space, grunting with the effort. His whole body flexed with the strain of lifting it off as he dragged it upwards and out of the top of Robert. The spirit roared.

Mark held on tightly and offered the now separated spirit a choice again. He waited, but ten seconds later the choice was made for him. Mark's guides came down on either side like two burly bouncers. They took hold of a spiritual arm each, and then they and Mark combined to push the spirit over to the light portal. Angrily, it struggled to get away, but after a few seconds the struggle diminished in intensity, changing to a half-hearted attempt at freedom. Mark saw why there was a slight change. Just inside the light portal were some white glowing forms with soft expressions, who emanated love. He knew instantly these were relatives of this ancestral spirit. They loved it and were waiting for it.

With a groan, the spirit was dragged over to their welcoming arms. Part of it wanted to go and felt relieved, while another part most certainly did not. You could feel the torn emotions as it was embraced by the waiting relatives with love and gratitude and drawn through the portal into the light. Then it was gone, and both portals vanished.

CHAPTER 15

ANCESTRAL CROSSROADS

DNA [noun]: Deoxyribonucleic Acid. DNA is thought to be the building block of life, the replicator. Spiritually, it is much more than that. It is like a tuning fork that resonates with similar life forces in the present, past, and future. We not only pick up wisdom and learnings from our ancestors but also their fears and unresolved karma.

With an audible sigh Mark relaxed, but the job was not done. He glanced around and saw they had still not been noticed by anyone else. He looked at Robert. 'It's gone, but I am not finished yet. There is still some negative residue left in you from where it was, and I need to clear it.'

Again Mark channelled energy through his body and out of his hands. He pushed healing white light into Robert's torso, starting at the heart and then working his way up and down. He felt some hooks left by the recently departed spirit, so he reached around either side of Robert's waist and, with the same twisting grabbing motion, pulled the roots up the side of his body and out of the top.

Hooks and roots attached to the body's auric field come in all shapes and sizes. They can appear in many forms, including needles, knives, darts, screws, or even planks, to name but a few.

He had even seen bands that look like chastity belts or like a worm burrowing deep inside. There really is no limit.

With his hands placed about Robert, he pulsed out healing cleansing white light, filling his body with it and burning away any dark residue that was left. Next, he dug an energetic trench in his torso and filled it with light, running centrally and vertically. Perfect.

When you remove something from the body like that, it leaves a hole in the energy field and aura. You have to fill that hole or gap. Otherwise it's like leaving an open wound with no bandage or antibiotics, and it can get re-infected and go bad. Finally, Mark held his hand over the heart itself, bathing and covering the heart space. He applied an energetic light plaster, closing and healing the hole that was in Robert and his aura.

Mark closed his eyes and called down a column of white light from above to surround and shield Robert, doing the same for himself. Then, speaking internally, he sent his thanks to his guides and all those that had helped him, asking for the healing to continue for Robert. Next he focused on himself and brought up energy from Mother Earth through his roots. He filled his body with her beautiful cleansing healing energy, until his body tingled all over and felt full to overflowing. He closed his chakras one by one and checked that his protective bubble was in place. Then he asked his guides to step back a little and opened his eyes.

'It's done,' he said. 'At least, the worst of it. You may still need to see me, but the main problem is removed.'

'Thanks,' Robert replied, somewhat shaken.

Mark stood and stretched. 'I need to go and wash my hands. I'll be back in a minute.'

He walked across the shop floor towards the toilets at the rear. It was only then he realised how much the clearing had taken out of him. He suddenly felt light-headed and weak. When he reached the washroom, he washed his hands and abruptly found himself leaning against the wall.

'Damn,' he thought. '*This is no place to remove nasty spirits from people! What was I thinking?*'

But he knew the answer even as he thought it. It had to be done, and if not him, who else was going to do it? He gathered himself and focused on his feet to shift his energy downwards and into the earth. He waited a minute and then went back to Anya and Robert, who were still waiting at the table.

As he sat down, he noticed two things immediately. Anya had bought him another tea. Second, and more importantly, Robert looked different—better and much lighter both physically and energetically. His skin colour appeared to have lightened, and the dark aura about him had vanished.

'How do you feel?' Mark asked.

He smiled. 'Good.'

'I can actually see a difference. He seems lighter. His skin looks better. You can see it in his face,' Anya said with a big smile. 'See, I said you needed to see Mark. You should have listened to me.'

'It's not done completely. You still need to see me again, but the worst is over.'

'So what was going on there?' Anya now had a serious look on her face.

Mark looked back to Robert. 'Well, it appears to have been your grandfather from your father's side. He was hooked into you, holding you back from your path and not doing you any favours at all.'

'Why would he do that?'

'He actually thought he was helping you in his own distorted way. You are not like your grandfather and other male relatives in the past. You're different, more caring and open. You have reached a crossroads here, Robert, a spiritual and self-developmental crossroads, breaking the mould of your ancestral line. Every now and then this happens. You get so many generations pass along, and then one person, linked by DNA, carries the torch and changes things for the good of all your line. Some hit major crossroads and others smaller ones. Some of the ancestors don't like this, as you are burning brighter than they ever will, and they try to prevent it. This is what he was doing. He's gone now. I sent him over into the light to continue his own evolution. He didn't like it, but he's gone to where he should be.'

'You look a little tired,' Anya said, looking at Mark with a concerned expression.

'Yes, it took a fair amount out of me. It's not exactly the perfect set up for spirit removal. The energies are all over the place in here, with hundreds of people walking through every day. Did you notice, though, that despite what I was doing, no one appeared to notice or pay us any attention at all? Not one person. It was like we weren't even here.'

They glanced around, and Anya said, 'You're right. They didn't seem to see us, did they?'

'No. My guides said they would deal with it. That's a first for me.'

'When can we see you again?'

'Not today. When did you have in mind? Sooner rather than later, I think.'

'Tomorrow?' she asked tentatively, knowing it was Sunday.

He thought for a second. 'Okay. Let's say ten o'clock? Just Robert, or you, or both of you?'

'Both, if you're up to it, please? We can come earlier if you want. Just text us in the morning. We are up at five o'clock anyway, and it would give you more of your Sunday free.'

'I'm sure it will be fine. Anyway, I think I need to go home to eat lunch and rest!'

'Sure. Thanks so much, Mark.'

Mark said his goodbyes and walked off.

CHAPTER 16

SUNDAY HEALING

Meditation [noun]: The state where we are awake, but where we get our inner chatter to abate, which allows us to recharge and access inner and outer wisdom and healing.

T he next day, the alarm went off at half past seven to give Mark time to prepare for Robert and Anya. She had mentioned they could come earlier if he wanted, so he sent a text suggesting he could be ready at nine o'clock. A few minutes later she responded, saying they would both be there at nine.

Mark jumped in the shower, where he relaxed and enjoyed the cleansing effect of hot water cascading down over him for several minutes. He towelled himself down and then threw on some jeans, a T-shirt, and a jumper. Refreshed and dressed, he walked downstairs into the kitchen and prepared himself some buckwheat porridge with organic sunflower seeds and blueberries, mixed in with a sprinkling of ground flax seeds. While the porridge heated up, he reflected on what had happened yesterday.

He felt revitalised this morning and fully recovered from yesterday's events in town. However, there would be more work to be done shortly. Robert would need to be finished, as his healing was not complete, but hopefully, it wouldn't take too much work, although, as always, he wouldn't know the complete picture until Robert was in front of him. It works like that. You can talk to spirit and tune in all you like, and, yes, you may get some answers and some clues, but you never really know fully until the person is right in front of you what you're going to do. Anya had stated that she also felt some problems, and, knowing the family history to date, he was prepared for just about anything.

He finished off his porridge and downed his vitamin tablets with a glass of filtered amethyst-energised water. Then he proceeded to wash the dishes, trying to calm his mind and prepare for the forthcoming healing. After that, he puttered around the house, tidying up a little and lighting some candles in the lounge and healing area, and then he sat down and meditated in a brown leather dining chair.

His living room had a light wood veneer floor and a cream leather sofa, adorned with burgundy cushions. Crystals were everywhere you looked. A glass rectangular dining table stood in the corner by the entrance, with specific healing crystals sitting on ribbed burgundy cloth mats. In the centre of the lounge was a low glass table standing on a flecked cream rug, with more crystals placed on another burgundy mat. Two large singing crystal bowls, used for sound therapy, sat comfortably underneath. In each corner of the room there were several glass shelves, also adorned with crystals. The lounge continued into a large conservatory, where, on the right, there was a wide wooden framed therapy couch used for healing. A chair was situated in the centre, and to the left was a large six-foot-long narrow table covered by a red silk cloth. The table was also covered in crystals of various sizes and hues. A large deeply coloured amethyst geode, probably weighing the better part of twenty-five kilos, sat prominently in the corner on the wooden floor. Amethyst is a great healer. Amongst other things, it helps to cleanse and anchor the energies in the room. All the various crystals around the room helped keep the energies clear and calm, creating a tranquil atmosphere that made the whole house feel like a sanctuary for all who walked in.

Mark switched on some Om Sanctuary background music, sat down in his chair, and deepened his meditation. He breathed deeply, sending his roots and energy down, grounding himself. He felt himself become clear and present. That sinking and heavy feeling settled on him as it always did, indicating he was connecting to Mother Earth. In return, she sent energies flowing up into him via his roots. He brought up violet light through the ground, raising it up into his house, gradually filling his home entirely. It brought a beautiful cleansed calm feeling to him, full of love and tranquillity.

He called in his guides and asked for their help in the healing to come. Some thirty minutes later he roused himself out of his meditative state and waited patiently for the doorbell to ring. Five minutes later, he opened the door to greet Anya and Robert, both smiling as always. He offered them a glass of water and waved them in and then walked through into the lounge.

Mark sat down and looked across at them both, now sitting comfortably on the sofa.

'How are you guys today? How are you feeling, Robert?'

'Good, actually. I slept well last night, which was nice.'

'Yes,' Anya said. 'He feels a lot better to me now as well.'

'Cool! Well, let's see what we need to do today. Yesterday I did just enough to leave you okay. Now I need to finish the job and remove any roots or negative energy left over and to see what else we can find. I can't see anything on you now, and you do look a lot lighter. I think what we'll do is take you into the healing room and leave Anya here. I don't think it will be a problem with both of you being here at the same time.'

Robert nodded in acquiescence, and Mark led him into the conservatory that served as his healing room and sat him in the chair. He pulled his guides in closer and reinforced his protection around both of them and the immediate vicinity. He placed his hands either side of Robert's head and channelled energy to feel what was going on. As he progressed, it turned out to be a relatively simple cleansing. He just needed to mop up the remaining negative energies and pull out the roots left from the spirit attachment. An hour later all was done.

Mark passed Robert a glass of water when he sat up, which he duly sipped.

'How do you feel, Robert?' he asked.

'Fine.' He looked around the room, eyes bright. 'Yes, I feel great, thanks.'

'Good! You look better, and everything is fine now. I removed any attachments and roots left by the spirit, cleared a few blockages, and generally cleansed you. Give yourself a few days while your body adjusts to the changes, but it should all be fine.'

Mark went into the kitchen to wash his hands. Once he had returned to the healing room, he called down some light and cleansed the area and himself in preparation for Anya. Satisfied, he called through.

'Okay, Anya, your turn. Ready?'

'Yes.'

She sat down in the chair in front of him, placing her hands in her lap, palms up.

'Mark, I know something is up. I had to see another healer while you were away, and he removed some things, but I still feel as though something is with me. I really feel it on my face, and I get head and neck aches too.'

'Okay, let's see what I find. Close your eyes and relax.'

He stood behind her and closed his eyes. Then he grounded again and called down his protection. He drew his guides closer, asking for their help and that of others who wanted to attend and were for her highest good. With his hands on either side of her head, he began to feel her energy and aura and tuned in to get a feel for what was going on. Channelling energy, he soon noticed there were some attachments and hooks on her and began the meticulous task of removing them. He used his hands to grab hold of an attachment around her brow, which felt like a layer of dark energy, a blanket if you like, and literally peeled it back and off. With a firm grip, he passed it behind him for his guides to take away.

When Mark had done this a few times, he moved to her throat and pulled out what appeared to be a long black plug of sorts. As he did so, he felt the root of the problem. A device had been placed in there and was causing her all kinds of difficulties. It was an energetic device, placed there by an ancestor to make life unpleasant and help provide a link to her ancestors. The net result made their attachment easier to maintain, feeding in more negativity.

He reached in hard, gave a surge of power, and pulled it out, passing it over to waiting guides to be disposed of. Then he pulled out the negative residue around the area and cleared it. Next he settled behind her and felt again. Immediately, he asked Anya to stand up. He reached with both hands round her lower abdomen and spine area where the base chakra is and took a firm grasp, pulling at the roots of another attachment. Mark dragged it up the centre of her body and over her head and lifted it off. For ten minutes, he lifted several layers off, clearing her body as he continued. Satisfied, he asked her to lie on the couch. Once she was lying on her back, he spoke again.

'Do you feel okay? I removed a device from your throat left there by an ancestor that was holding you back and I also removed a lot from your head and body.'

'Yes,' she replied, 'I felt it, but I still feel something is there.'

'I know. We are removing layers, and we'll get to the root of this. Close your eyes and relax.'

The attachments, entities, and hooks that he removed, depending what they specifically were, would be taken to a place best suited for them in their realm and for their highest good. Sometimes it would be an ancestor or earthbound spirit that just needed to be passed over into the light to continue its own journey. Sometimes it was a dark being that needed to return to its own home and plane of existence. Sometimes it was just negative energy that could be transmuted into positive energy and released into the universe.

Positioned alongside the couch, Mark placed his hands, palms towards her, slightly raised from his sides, and channelled energy. He directed the energy towards Anya and encased her in an energy field. He sent his attention over her face and thought he felt something—something not quite right. He stepped in closer and peered into her, feeling, looking for something untoward.

Suddenly, two yellow slanted eyes miraculously appeared in her face! Taken aback, he looked again. There was no doubt. Clear as day now, he could see two yellow slanted eyes right in front of him, sitting right inside her face. No wonder she felt bad. He could feel the waves of negativity emanating from this entity. He paused for a second as realisation struck. No, this was not just an entity, but a full-fledged demon! A powerful one at that.

He stood back slightly and steeled himself, drawing all the energy he could muster and reinforcing his shields. His guides needed no prompting, and he felt the reassuring presence of his two main guides, large powerful beings, drawing closer to him, one on either side. Others stepped in and lent their strength. He had whole teams working for him, but it wasn't going to be enough. When Mark realised that, he sent his thoughts up, asking directly for Archangel Michael, the strongest angel in God's armoury, Archangel Michael specialised in these matters, and one of his roles was to come and help when needed for scenarios such as this.

Mark felt rather than saw him as he immediately appeared in the room. He appeared as a tall masculine being wearing armour and carrying a massive broadsword in his right hand. He stood on the opposite side of the couch above the floor. A blue nimbus light surrounded him, which permeated through his entire being. The sheer presence of this archangel was overwhelming.

Without being told, Mark knew instinctively what to do. He held the energies in the room and around the couch. Michael reached in with one hand and grasped the demon inside her. It screamed its rage, but it was no match for the archangel. The demon was relentlessly drawn out in seconds, grasped firmly in one powerful hand. Held in impotent rage, its shapeless dark form squirmed and writhed to no avail. Yellow eyes stared at Michael as its negative radiance was counteracted by Michael's blue aura. Michael reached to his side and drew his massive broadsword. Several feet in length, he held it out, and it glowed a bright pale blue. The demon's demeanour suddenly changed. It realised its plight, and its struggles intensified as it realised there was no escape. Then it shrank back in desperation, frantically trying to pull away from the glowing sword that filled its entire vision. Its yellow eyes darted from side to side as it dawned on it that something was wrong. It wouldn't just be sent away back to the underworld. This was death.

Michael's blue aura brightened, and he raised his arm. With a giant sweeping arc that started above his head and a chilling hissing sound, he swept the broadsword down from right to left, cutting straight through the demon, literally severing it in half, like a knife through butter. Mark stood stock still, transfixed by the scene before his eyes. The archangel pulled his sword back and cut through the body again. The demon cried in anguish, screaming its pain. Relentlessly, Michael continued cutting the demon to pieces. Slowly, the screams died, to be replaced with complete and utter silence, a silence which was as devastating to hear as the screams had been only moments before. The pieces that had formed the demon dissipated, vanishing before Mark's eyes.

Totally unprepared for what he had just witnessed, Mark stood dumbstruck. This wasn't the way things would normally be dealt with. He had expected the demon to just be sent back to whence it came, not cut to pieces. Everything wasn't what it seemed.

Michael looked at him. *'This was an experience for you to learn. This is what I can do. Such is my power. You needed to see what I can do so you could understand. It is not always like this. I have worked with you before, but never in this manner, and you needed a greater understanding of the bigger picture. It is not just about what I can do but an experience in the forces around you.'*

'So all this was just so I could learn?' Mark asked.

'Yes. It would not normally be done this way. I could have just sent him to his realm to answer to his own hierarchy, but everything is as it should be, and this was necessary. You can finish healing now. The demon is gone.'

With a gentle smile he stepped back and vanished. Mark took stock of what had happened. Still stunned by events, he refocused on Anya and continued healing. He addressed the demon's residue that was left in her energy fields, carefully found all the roots and hooks that remained, and removed them one by one. There were holes in her aura where the demon and its negative energy had been residing. As he channelled light out of his hands, he filled the holes and repaired her aura, bathing her entire body in white light. He stood this way for several minutes until he was satisfied the job was done. Then he connected with Mother Earth, who sent a beautiful pink light that encased Anya in a glowing nimbus which permeated her entire being. Mark closed her chakras individually and then surrounded her in white light as a final protective barrier.

'Anya,' he said gently, placing his hand on her shoulder. She opened her eyes and smiled. 'How do you feel?'

'Amazing,' she replied. 'I could feel you remove something from my face, and I feel so much better now.'

'I had some help.' Mark smiled.

'Is it gone?'

'Yes, it's gone and won't return.'

CHAPTER 17

THE SUMMONS

The group had moved from their usual spot in the clouds. They had found themselves summoned and were currently sitting in a white marble room somewhere in the etheric fields. No one knew exactly where except those who had created the space—the archangels.

Nervously, they waited in expectation. Three high-ranking angels sat behind a white marble desk looking at something that appeared to be a manuscript of some description. The middle one of the three looked up, staring intently at all three of them. All three light beings shifted uncomfortably. Only Red Shaman seemed to hold his own, looking back defiantly at them.

'*We don't appreciate being used like that. What you did was against protocol.*'

'*It was necessary. We have to adapt and evolve as he passes his tests. It is vital when training our warriors. As he moves and shifts, we must too. You understand as well as we do how important his training is,*' Red Shaman replied.

'*That may be so,*' the central angel said. Clearly he was the one acting as spokesperson over the proceedings. '*But protocol is there for a reason, and it is not to be breached when or how you see fit!*'

'*This was just. You know what's at stake. He must be ready to join the others. We have so little time. How can he be ready if we don't do what we do?*'

'*What do you mean, ready?*'

'*Ah, so you don't know everything then. Our group works in secret for a reason. We don't answer to you.*'

The angel gasped in outrage.

Quickly Red Shaman held up his hand in a conciliatory gesture.

'*It is not our intention to offend, but not everyone can know what we do all the time, not even the archangels. They have their own role. We are acting under Supreme Authority, and I apologise for any slight caused. It was necessary.*'

The three angels looked at each other and reached an unspoken agreement. The central angel turned about and addressed them once more.

'*Very well. We acquiesce. But let it be known that we desire no further incursions into our authority without prior request.*' He paused, allowing his words to sink in. '*You may go.*'

The three light beings stood up and bowed low. As one, they turned and exited the room through the light door and instantly found themselves in the clouds where they had been prior to the summoning.

'*That was unpleasant,*' Malek said. '*I'd rather not have to go through that again.*'

The other two nodded.

Red Shaman said, '*Now they know who we serve and that we have little choice, let's hope we have no more interference. We have better things to do than answer summons from bureaucrats with ruffled feathers.*'

CHAPTER 18

MOTHER, FATHER, AND BROTHER

Elemental [noun]: An inhabitant of the lower planes beneath our three dimensions. These beings can be helpful and magical but also naughty and mischievous.

T wo weeks later Anya called Mark on the phone and said she was experiencing some other symptoms and still felt a presence inside her. She had developed a bizarre desire to eat red meat, which she would never normally touch. She had put on a stone in weight in the last fortnight alone. The entity in her was whispering things in her mind, telling her to eat and keeping her up at night. She wasn't afraid, but she needed it removed. She also asked Mark if another medium she knew could attend. She explained that he had met her before one time when they were having coffee in Howden's.

Mark remembered the woman. She was in her early thirties, tall with a very slim build and short blond hair. She had a presence about her, a very light energy that shone out like a beacon. Picture fairies with that soft white glow around them, and that would be close to what she looked and felt like. He had spoken to her for a while. She was naturally gifted, receiving messages as pictures and symbols. She really was very good, he seemed to remember. One of those natural mediums that just are.

She was unwilling to dabble in the dark side of the spirit world though. Instead she represented a beacon of light, playing only in the light like a pond fairy skimming over the top of the surface, just dipping her toes in as she travelled, spreading cheer and goodwill wherever she went. We all have our path to follow and roles to perform. Each and every one of us contributes somehow to the world. While Mark was prepared to delve in the dark, digging deep down into the earth and elemental realms, she stayed in the light above, barely touching the ground. All was in balance.

Mark hesitated only momentarily before he agreed. Anya said they would both be at her home when he came over next Friday morning.

The next two days passed quickly, and he soon found himself sitting in Anya's lounge with the young medium. He'd remembered she was called Tracey. She lounged on a sofa while Anya ushered him through a doorway into the kitchen. Introductions were exchanged, and Anya told Mark what was happening.

As he listened to her narration, a vision suddenly appeared in his mind. A group of what looked like black voodoo witch doctors were sitting in a hut in a jungle somewhere. There were three of them, sitting cross-legged on a hard packed mud floor around a burning fire in the centre of the hut. They all sported bone necklaces of animal teeth and scant loin cloths with some fur about them. Tattoos were evident on areas of exposed flesh. There was a dark feel to them, and he knew beyond doubt that dark energy was being used here for sinister purposes. Unlike his own use of the dark side for the higher good, these people worked with the dark for their own evil agenda. They were the ones responsible for sending dark goings on to Anya.

Mark turned back towards Anya as she continued to describe what Tracey had told her. As the narrative unfolded, it became apparent that Tracey had seen exactly the same as he had in his vision only minutes before. Three witch doctors were sitting in a hut, conducting dark summonings and rituals and sending over these entities from the demonic realm to plague Anya. Just then he realised what he had only suspected moments before. These three witch doctors were representing Anya's brother, father, and mother, who were the originators of the attacks. His conclusions were verified moments later by Anya.

Turning to Tracey, he asked what she had seen.

'I saw these witch-doctor-type men in a hut, three of them. Each of them represented one of her family—her father, mother, and brother,' she said.

Thoughtfully, Mark replied. 'Yes, that's what I saw too. They are the ones that your family are going to, Anya, to send over these demons and cause you all these problems.'

'I know. I hadn't realised my mother was doing it as well though. I always got on well with her, and I speak to her regularly on the phone. Recently, though, she has been a bit distant with me. Now I guess I know why,' she replied with a wistful look.

He turned to Tracey. 'What else?'

'I've seen three entities in her, one female and two male, I think. One of them is deeper than the others and has been around a long time but keeps hiding. The others are newer.'

After mulling it over for a few seconds, he realised that each of these also represented one of the members of her family.

He looked around the room and noticed that a therapy couch had been erected in the corner. He had missed this as he walked in. He pulled it over to the centre and laid a folded white sheet on top over the surface. Then he brought one of her heavy ornate wooden chairs from the large table in the dining room and placed it close to the couch.

'Mark, do you mind if I play my Hindu prayer music? They hate it, and it'll make them easier to remove.'

'Sure.'

Anya set up her iPad to play some Hindu prayers, and the chanting came alive as she sat down on the chair. She chanted the same Hindu prayer, holding some prayer beads around her neck and a white shawl over her shoulders with her head bowed down. The energy shifted in the room and became almost intimidating, what with the Hindu prayer music and Anya's chanting and appearance as she played with her beads. The young medium sat with tense anticipation on the sofa while Mark stood ready to perform some rites. It created a macabre scene to any would-be observer.

He glanced over at Tracey and saw a look of trepidation cross her features. He told her to keep back a little but said she was free to watch and tell him things she saw if she felt they were important.

'But you had better set up your protections and call your guides in. I'll make sure you're protected also, but you still should make sure your guides step in,' he said.

With a nod, Tracey stood back, and he received a sense of her own guides moving closer. He called in his own, brought his protections in place, and pulled off tendrils of dark matter from Anya's energy field. He disposed of them in energy waste bins which miraculously appeared wherever he needed them. Within minutes, a male entity appeared over her right shoulder, just standing there motionless. Mark stepped behind and took hold of it and held it fast, bracing himself to pull the entity off Anya and hand it over to waiting higher beings for them to deal with. Although it was not a good spirit, so to speak, the entity was still a human spirit and would be taken to the light and dealt with by the powers that be. He summoned a gateway for its entrance to the light realms and manoeuvred it into position, and with a gentle push it went through.

One down. It was likely there would be more, so he continued clearing for several minutes until he noticed that another male spirit that was not meant to be there was attached lightly behind her. As before, he reached over and took hold of this new male spirit to hold it securely. With a small yank of his arms, he pulled it off her and passed it towards the waiting gateway, where his guides and other spiritual helpers took over, leading it through to the other side.

So far the spirits had been relatively easy to remove. He didn't think they'd had time to solidify themselves into Anya's aura. Having said that, you might feel he was making it look easier than it was. Like all things, it varies, but generally speaking, you can be assured it is not simple. If they do not wish to go and are firmly entrenched into the person's aura it is most definitely not easy to remove spirits. It requires a large amount of energy, much as you would need if you were pushing a very heavy object or trying to pull someone who did not wish to be pulled in the material world. The harder and more powerful the being you are trying to move on or remove, the more power is required. You can end up with almost a tug of war and be exhausted at the end.

Tracey gave him a nod when he looked over at her. 'I saw those two. They were quite amazing really. I can almost feel the lightness around now.'

During the healing and lifting, Anya's chanting had sped up, and she had become much more intense, and the energy in the room became more intense with her. Mark placed his hands about her again and continued channelling energy, lifting off negative attachments and hooks left by the two spirits he had just moved over to the light.

Now he picked up a sense of something else that was deeper and nastier than the other two. This posed significantly more of a challenge than the former entities he had just disposed of. Mark focused his attention right behind Anya. He glanced again at Tracey for confirmation of what he already knew.

'There is something else here. This one is female, I think, and much deeper too. It's almost like she is right inside her.'

He took hold of a negative band of energy on each side of her and dragged a layer up and over, passing it across to be taken away by his waiting guides. He repeated this several times, stood back, and took a spiritual look around Anya, who had now started crying, tears running down her cheeks. The vibration in the room had increased and felt electric.

The Hindu chanting rose in volume. Anya now stood with her head bowed, frantically playing with her prayer beads whilst chanting a prayer. This created a dramatic scene. Mark stood over her with hands outstretched and a determined look on his face, pulling entities off her. It was like something out of a horror movie.

Acutely aware of Anya's discomfort, he glanced over at Tracey, who was wide-eyed and looked quite lost. Still standing slightly back, he channelled light into her for a few moments more. To his surprise, Anya spontaneously began to slap herself about the face. She started slowly at first, but the slaps gathered in pace and force at an alarming rate. Tracey took hold of her hands, and Anya's cries and sobs rapidly turned into screams and wailing.

Mark held the energy, trying to get to the root of the problem, and allowed Tracey to console and support her. But Anya was having none of it. She shook her hands free and slapped herself even harder. She was close to injuring herself significantly with the viciousness of it. Enough was enough. Mark took hold of the offending hands and held them both fast.

'That's enough,' he snapped. 'No more. I won't allow you to do that. Now stop.'

'But I can't help it,' she wailed. 'It's making me do it!'

'That's enough.' he said again, raising his voice. It seemed he had pierced through her trance-like state, and her hands grew still in his.

'Give me a minute and I'll get rid of this thing, but no more hitting yourself,' he said.

Still holding her hands for a few seconds more, he stepped back.

CHAPTER 19

GUARDIAN OF THE UNDERWORLD

Exorcism [noun]: The process of casting out demonic possessions. In these cases the demon has to envisage a power similar to it but more forceful in order to leave.

M ark knew at once that this entity was significantly different, steeped in evil and insidiously entwined into Anya's very being. He could see its main body and limbs, flowing and pulsing, firmly attached but constantly moving. This was not going to be easy. Quickly he decided to call in a helper from the underworld who would be able to deal with it.

So far (barring his dark guides) the only other he had seen that was meant to work with him had been an intermediary dark underworld guardian. Mark knew he was not the big boss, so to speak, but he had only received glimpses of the real powerful dark being who was waiting to show himself. He had obviously been waiting for the right time. And this was it.

Mark called him forward. At first he sensed only his intermediary underworld guardian. He was humanoid in shape but with some distinct differences. The upright horns that adorned the top of his head were three or four inches high, and small but sharp pointed teeth filled his mouth. There was an entirely different aura about him also—darker, like looking at light through a darkened lens.

Moments later an enormous presence rose up about six feet behind him. Its sheer presence and power were staggering, and Mark took an involuntary step forward. My god, it was scaring even him. Totally black in colour, it had a head with ram's horns on the top and a jaw with fangs that could just be seen between a lipless mouth, fixed in a grimace. Long muscular arms with talons for fingers hung either side of a thick muscular torso. Legs like tree trunks supported its massive bulk. It took a step forward and paused, waiting, emanating power and intimidation.

Mark gathered his wits and acknowledged his new dark guardian. Then he spoke to the entity attached to Anya. *'It is time for you to leave. You are no longer wanted or needed. You can see who is behind me. You can do this the easy way or the hard way. It is your choice, but either way you will be leaving.'*

The situation had changed drastically for the unwanted entity. It was no longer dealing with just Mark and expecting to fight. The balance had just massively tipped in Mark's favour, and the odds for it weren't good. He could sense the shift in its energy and the uncertainty now coming across. For a few seconds he waited, allowing it time to make a decision. It didn't. Mark made the decision for it.

'Fine, you had your chance.'

He instantly brought in his energy and called forward the dark gate keeper behind him who was one of the 'big guns' from the underworld. He was a demon lord in his own right. Mark wasn't really sure exactly what to expect when he called him forward, because it can often go several different ways. But the demon lord decided to use him as a vessel and stepped right into him. He stepped out of his body at once to make room for it, allowing his spirit and consciousness to move aside, temporarily granting the use of his physical body.

Its presence was huge, and a feeling of power flowed through Mark as it took control of his physical body and moved him forward. The rush was intoxicating and almost overpowering.

Although he had temporarily relinquished self-control, he was still aware of everything that occurred, and part of him revelled in this newfound power. It was as though he'd been injected with a massive adrenalin and testosterone mix. The hybrid of Mark and the demon lord stepped up to Anya with outstretched arms.

He took hold of the entity on both sides with a massively powerful grip and surged upwards, dragging it off and out of her. The entity had no chance—none at all. With the uninvited guest firmly in his grasp, he stomped around to where the dark lord had first arisen from its portal to the Underworld and released all control of Mark's physical body. Its true form reappeared, and Mark watched the dark lord drop down through the open black portal from whence it had come, dragging the hapless entity with him.

Mark regained control of his senses and physical body as he watched the Demon Lord disappear below. He took a few moments to thank him and, as the portal winked shut, he experienced a slight pang of regret to lose the power he had just experienced. Then he closed the path to the underworld, turned back to Anya, and looked carefully at her.

It was gone.

He channelled light into her and cleared leftover dark residue. Then he noticed in his peripheral vision some shadow-like figures a few feet away in the kitchen. They were just standing there, floating above the ground, dark and humanoid in shape, watching the scene. He hadn't seen them before, and he knew they weren't spirits. Upon closer inspection, he realised they were spectres or shadows of the three witch doctors who had sent over the recent entities he had just removed. They were watching, learning, and feeding back information.

Mark stepped towards them. With a flick of his hand and force of energy and intent, the first one vanished. The other two quickly followed suit, one after the other, until all three had disappeared from sight. A feeling of intense surprise wafted over him from the spectres as they vanished. Clearly they believed they had been unobserved and invisible to him. Now they were aware that Anya had help, and powerful help at that.

Anya sagged and Mark moved over to her.

'Are you okay? How do you feel now?'

'Lighter, better, thanks. Has it gone?'

'Yes, it's done. Take a seat over here and I'll get you some water.'

She sat down next to Tracey on the sofa. Mark returned with a glass of water and passed it to Anya, looking carefully at her. She definitely looked lighter of spirit and colour. He could feel nothing untoward anymore. Tracey still looked a little wild-eyed from what she had just witnessed, and she answered his questioning expression with a shake of her head in the negative. She couldn't sense anything now either.

As Anya recovered, Mark explained what he had seen and done, leaving almost nothing out. Her face was a mask of incredulity as she listened.

'Mark,' she said. 'I just couldn't stop myself. It was forcing me to hit myself. It was horrible.'

'I know. It's gone now, and they know about me too—that you have help, powerful help. They were very surprised when I sent back their shadows. They didn't think I could see them, never mind send them back. That will give them something to think about. They are running out of options, and I think you will find things improve a lot now.'

'I hope so, because I can't take much more of this.'

'You won't have to. Trust me. It will all start to improve. We have broken their hold over you, and nothing else will be as bad. Call me if you have any more problems. You know where I am.'

With that, Mark got up and gathered his belongings. After putting on his shoes in the hallway, he opened the front door to leave. He gave both Anya and Tracey a parting hug and walked out into the street.

As he climbed into his car and gunned the engine, he thought about what had happened since he met Anya that fateful day in the summer of the previous year at his Platform event. Who would have thought her request for help would lead to this wild terrifying ride? Even he was amazed. At times it felt like something out of *The Exorcist*. It even looked like it. Bad demons, good demons, underworld guardians, dark guides, entity possession, werewolves, and dark plots by evil witch doctors in far off countries. All hired by vengeful family members to bring unhappiness and ruin. It was almost beyond belief.

But he still sensed this was not to be the end of it. And he was right.

CHAPTER 20

DESTINY

The three of them stood together once more in their cloudy meeting spot. Half in, half out, they enjoyed the peace, solitude, and privacy of meeting in the skies above. They could, if necessary, travel anywhere, but this was an easier place to reach, being neither fully on the earthly plane nor in spirit but somewhere in between.

'His training is progressing well. Events are moving according to plan. Our forefathers will be pleased,' Malek said.

'Indeed,' replied Red Shaman. 'Things are moving according to plan. But in this phase of time we must be swift to be ready; else all will be out of sync. The final part of his training must be put into place before he can be ready for the next phase. Let us complete this scenario.'

Abatheer, not usually known for cautiousness or more intricate planning, spoke. 'Are you sure he is ready? Even though time runs away, if we place him too early, all will be amok.'

'He is ready. Engage the final scenario. Initiate the physical astral projection engagement. If he fails this we will know,' said Red Shaman.

With a nod, the two light beings vanished, leaving Red Shaman standing in the clouds alone. He put his concerns to one side and whispered on the breeze. 'All will be well, brave one. Complete what you are destined to do.'

Once more Red Shaman uttered a curse in that language not heard for over a million years. With a flash, three random Light Beings from his Order morphed into witch doctors.

Red Shaman watched as seconds later their forms, now dark, streamed down to the earth plane, trailing black energetic residue.

CHAPTER 21

THE FINAL RAID

Manifestation [noun]: The ability of humans, as conscious self-aware beings, to manifest their thought forms into the physical plane. Other animals and plants also contribute to the world we live in, but in more subtle ways.

A month or so later Mark received another call from Anya asking him to come over. She had problems again. So it was that he found himself walking into her house in a now all-too-familiar scenario, sitting opposite her, and preparing to hear the latest instalment to this saga.

As always, prior to this kind of work going into somebody's house, he would prepare himself. Particularly where Anya was concerned, he knew it would likely be serious.

He gave her his full attention as he listened to what she had to say, while at the same time focusing both on her energies and on his environment. She told him it felt as though she had another attachment and could feel them attacking her. He didn't need to ask who, but he did anyway just for confirmation. It was the same people as before, in India, the three witch doctors. She explained that she felt her family were still very much behind it all. After listening to her for five minutes and sipping the tea she had brought him when he entered, he got up and asked her to sit in the heavy ornate wooden chair she had placed in the centre of the lounge.

He stood behind Anya when she sat down, asking for help and guidance to heal and whatever else needed to be done. Again he called his protection around him and tuned in. Then he placed his hands about her head and felt what was happening within her energy fields. Almost immediately he felt various blockages and attachments located in different areas around her. As he worked through the superficial layers about her throat, he took hold of a particularly nasty choker-like collar from her neck and pulled it off, dumping it in the spiritual waste bin he had placed beside him. He proceeded to remove different layers from her neck, shoulders, and torso. All of them appeared to have been recently attached.

'They aren't giving up, are they?' he said to Anya.

'No. Will it ever stop, Mark?'

'It will, but it's an ongoing process. Part of this journey is for you to learn from. We are getting on top of it though, and these attachments are recent.'

A scene then appeared in his mind, a vision of sorts. In it he saw three witch doctors sitting in a large native-style hut. A fire burned in the centre, and they appeared to be surrounded by various witchcraft paraphernalia. Smoke rose from the fire, giving the interior an eerie look. He realised the hut was somewhat larger than he had first thought, maybe fourteen foot in length by ten foot wide. It was hard to tell. He was more interested in the fact that he felt as though he was actually there with them in spirit form, rather than viewing them from afar.

Reality dawned moments later. He was there! His spirit-self had actually travelled across the globe and was looking around the hut directly. This was not just simple astral projection. He was physically there and could act accordingly, altering things in this space-time reality if necessary.

The three witch doctors had very dark energy about them, and he felt evil voodoo magic in the air. Events unfurled rapidly from that point on, as the witch doctors turned around in unison and looked at him. He felt a sense of righteousness as his main guides flowed through his essence. More of his spiritual guardians flanked his sides, and he stared at the three witch doctors. It was barely his thoughts or voice as he spoke in a low, flint-like tone.

'Stop this now! No more! She is under my protection.'

A look of surprise covered their features, followed swiftly by resentment and outrage mixed with fear. Instantly he knew he was about to be attacked. They proceeded to mouth unrecognisable words and incantations. Dark energy spirit forms materialised around them to confront Mark and his guides. The guides recognised the imminence of battle and stepped in closer to strengthen their position within him. Ranks of light and dark spirit beings faced each other, appearing at will out of thin air, silent, yet menacing. Moments passed.

Then the standoff broke and opposing spiritual forms flew at one another in a silent crash of energy. Mark stepped forward towards the closest witch doctor and struck him to the ground with a single blow. A sense of outrage came over him, and with a sweeping gesture of his arm, the other two swiftly followed suit.

Mark picked up the first one by the throat and pinned him against the wall, lifting him up until his feet dangled six inches above the floor. Helplessly pinned by a strength he couldn't hope to match, the witch doctor struggled futilely and then went limp. Then, turning towards the other two, Mark pointed his fingers to where they now stood, dazed and trying to hide behind a pillar at the back of the hut. His meaning and warning very clear: stay out of it and stay put.

Light and dark forms continued their silent struggle for dominance. The energy was rife, crackling with menace and aggression, weaving and bucking as the silent battle raged. More dark energy forms appeared, and a greater number of light forms materialised to counteract them. Dozens of beings on both sides now tussled in the air.

As the battle raged about him, Mark left the beleaguered witch doctor pinned up against the wall with an energetic hand clasped firmly around his throat. He felt a rage building within, gathering quickly in intensity until it reached a climax. He galvanised himself into action and felt himself, eyes blazing, go on a rampage in the hut. Stomping across the floor, he systematically pulled down anything within reach. Shelves filled with jars and objects attached to their craft were dashed to the ground. He kicked things over, tipping their contents to the floor and generally wrecking anything he could see. Mark's seething fury was tangible. He spied a cauldron cooking over the fire in the centre of the hut, strode towards it and, with a hefty kick, booted it off its supporting tripod. The water and contents spilled over the fire, dowsing it with a large hiss. Flames died as sparks and steam leapt into the air in protest above the dowsed fire.

The tide was slowly turning in his favour, and he moved over to the witch doctor who was still pinned helplessly against the wall.

'*That's enough.*' He tightened his grip on the spirit's throat. There was a spark of defiance in the witch doctor's eyes, and then they dropped, looking at the floor. The dark forms were now secured, standing stationary with light beings about them, effectively detained and under arrest.

The other two witch doctors were still standing where he had left them, in apparent surrender. The one he had in front of him, clearly the dominant of the three, still had an air of defiance. Obviously, he had to do more. Without his asking, two angels appeared, hovering above the hut. Their glowing white forms were clearly visible as they projected light out of their hands into the hut. Then more angels appeared, until a full dozen floated above the hut, light bursting forth from their hands and filling the hut with a white brilliance. The intensity increased to such a degree that, had Mark been there in real physical form, he would have been forced to cover his eyes lest he be potentially struck blind. He sensed an even higher level being must be supporting this angelic host. Just then, a brief vision of Archangel Michael appeared above the angels. He had sent them and was taking a hand in this himself. The light pierced every particle within the hut, burning away all residue of dark energy. At that point, the dark beings suddenly vanished, leaving only light guardians standing inside. An almost unnatural stillness replaced the chaotic energy that had been there only a few minutes before.

Mark turned his attention back to the main witch doctor and leaned in closer. Within a few inches of his face, he spoke in an ominous tone.

'That's enough! This ends now! She is under my protection.'

The witch doctor looked around. His hut was a shambles. Pots, ornaments, and paraphernalia littered the floor. Shelves hung askew off walls, and items smashed on the walls and floor were strewn about him. It looked like a hurricane had hit. He had been seriously out-gunned by Mark's overwhelming forces, along with the intervention of the angels and Archangel Michael himself. A mixture of fear, awe, and acquiescence shone in his eyes. With a nod of his head, he gave his submission.

Mark could feel the presence of his guides within him. Still outraged with what had transpired and the actions of the dark witch doctors, he spoke with determination and resolve. His voice dripped with venom and was barely recognisable as his own.

'This is to stop. No more. If I have to come back here again, it will be a different story, and you won't like it. They are under my protection now, and you will leave them alone. You've seen what happened today. Don't make me come back again.'

Mark released him, and he dropped to the floor. With a gesture of his hand, he moved the witch doctor over to his confederates.

Mark returned to his body, which was still standing behind Anya. His mind boggled as he realised what had just happened—a full-on battle between light and dark on a completely different plane of existence. Not only that, he had also travelled over in spirit form to a location in another country on the other side of the globe and had actually been able to manipulate events, both physical and spiritual, while there.

He gave himself a few moments to gather his thoughts, ground himself, and focus on the task in hand. Then he continued the healing but found there was nothing serious left on Anya. After he finished, she asked him what happened. He sat down, and a feeling of exhaustion washed over him. He launched into the story without embellishment and recounted the battle to her. Her eyes widened as the tale unfolded.

'I don't think they will be so keen to rush into things with you now. We've given them something serious to think about. I'm not sure it will totally be the end of it all, but we have just won a major victory. They are now on the back foot in a big way. Let me know what happens over the next few days, and stay in touch.'

Mark left the house again and drove home. He felt exhausted. He hadn't realised how much that battle would take out of him.

Spirit had upped the game with him, and he was being given bigger things to do. Dark energy was being used for malicious purposes, serving petty human emotions such as malice, jealousy, greed, and hatred. Someone has to counteract that force in the physical world, and he guessed he'd been chosen as one of the people to do it. He mulled over what he had learned on this journey and that final realisation of his role.

'Yes,' he thought. *I'm happy with that.*

As he drove, he looked forward to getting some rest time, but the powers that be had other ideas. A silent shift in the coalition of realms across the universe could be sensed by those so attuned. Another part of the never-ending universal plan clicked into place. The job was not yet done.

CHAPTER 22

DAYLIGHT AMBUSH

Soldier Guide [noun]: A spiritual being providing a more specific role in their support of us while we are in physical form.

Two days later Mark received a message on his phone from Anya, inviting him to stay at their townhouse in London to relax for a few days. Technically, the property was owned by her cousin, but they all used it when they wished, and her cousin was away. The house was only used by Robert on business stays in London or when the family wanted a change of scenery for the weekend or such.

He thought about it briefly and decided it would be a good idea to have a break and change of scenery. He messaged back his grateful acceptance and received the address, along with a cart-blanche to use the house as he chose. He looked at his diary and saw that he had the following weekend clear and mentally booked it.

Wondering what the property looked like, he went upstairs to his computer. Google and modern search engines are marvellous tools, and within a couple of minutes he'd found the house on line. Situated on an urban street in inner London, the house was three stories high and appeared Victorian. Long and narrow with high chimneys, the property seemed well maintained on the outside. The standard sash windows for that period were prominent, and the house appeared to have a basement too. Anya had told him there were allocated parking bays outside, and he could see them in the photo, so driving would be no problem.

His curiosity temporarily sated, Mark switched off the computer and prepared for an early night. Still feeling tired from previous events, he knew how important it was to recharge his energies. Lying in bed a short time later, he felt himself drifting off to sleep, looking forward to a nice break in London. However, as it turned out, that was not to be the case.

The weekend came surprisingly quickly, and Mark found himself in the car driving to the townhouse, happy at the prospect. As he approached the inner areas of London, traffic slowed down somewhat, and Mark sat listening to the music system in his car, becoming slightly frustrated with the journey as time dragged by. Horns started to honk as other drivers expressed their own frustration at the delays. Some thirty minutes later the cause of the delays became apparent as road works materialised ahead, funnelling everything down to one lane and a contraflow traffic system with temporary traffic lights. He eventually made it past the road works as the road cleared, and he made the rest of the journey in good time, arriving some twenty minutes later in the middle of the afternoon.

The sat nav took him right to the front door. There were clearly marked parking bays directly outside the house. Although he was feeling jaded and a little distracted, he unloaded his boot and removed the holdall full of clothes and other necessities. It was perhaps for this reason as he opened the front door that he missed the face shrouded in darkness looking out of the top floor window.

Entering the house, he saw a long hallway immediately in front of him and a staircase leading upstairs directly ahead. The walls were painted in magnolia, and the hall smelt of recent decoration.

Dropping his bag on the floor he decided to have a look around. Along the hallway there was a door on the left leading to a double lounge area. The first part opened to the front, with large sash windows and deep brown curtains. A couple of sofas were evident, and a large flat screen television sat on a stand in the corner. A few pictures hung on the walls. One in particular drew his attention. A river town scene from a few centuries ago, clearly Hispanic in origin, painted predominantly in browns, oranges, and reds. It didn't look right. It didn't feel right either. Pushing it to the back of his mind, Mark turned into the second part of the lounge.

Old-style French doors graced the rear of the property, opening up into the garden. Walking over, he looked into the back garden, which was typically small for this style of house in London, perhaps fifteen foot wide by thirty foot long. From the doors, a paved area merged into a pathway leading towards a water feature at the centre, with gravel and shrubbery on either side. Beyond the stone water fountain feature was a small grassed area with a wooden bench to one side and flower beds around the edges. A pretty shed was situated in one corner, freshly painted with wood sealant to a deep oak brown. Someone had put a lot of love into this garden.

Leaving the garden view, he walked out of the lounge and turned left into the kitchen. Old-style wooden units adorned the walls and floor, and there was a stairway in the corner. Mark strode over to the stairway and looked down. It clearly led to a basement. He descended the first few steps, flicking the light switch on as he went. A single light bulb flared to life. Peering around the side wall, he saw that it was largely empty except for a bed pushed head first against the rear wall. A few chests of draws sat opposite. It wasn't the most inviting of rooms. Having seen enough, he walked back up and decided to take his bag upstairs.

At the bottom of the stairs, bag in hand, he stopped. Looking up he saw nothing, but still his senses had suddenly become fully alert. Something was wrong. Dropping his bag to the floor, he stared at the top of the steep narrow stairs. There was a small landing before the stairs banked up and to the left. A window lit the stairway from above, with some small animal ornaments and a pot plant sitting on the sill. An eerie intermittent scraping sound suddenly broke the silence. It appeared to be coming from up the stairs. Mark scanned upwards, looking for the source of the sound. His eyes caught a slight movement. The pot plant was sliding towards the edge of the sill all on its own! No obvious cause was visible, and the window was a non-opening one. No draughts or breath of air could be felt.

It paused momentarily in its movement and teetered on the edge. Apparently of its own violation, the pot plant suddenly lurched forward, tipping over the edge, and flew down the stairs, shattering with a loud crack halfway down as plant, earth, and pottery exploded on impact, bouncing down the stairs with far more force than would be normal. It splashed the wall and stairway with a mixture of earth, plant, and clay on its rapid descent.

Mark stood mesmerised as the pot and its contents hurtled towards him. He couldn't believe what he was seeing! At the last second he stepped aside, and the last parts of the shattered pot and its contents soared past his head. He felt the rush of air past his ear as it narrowly missed him, finally coming to rest with shattering impact on the floor several feet behind him.

Silence descended. He looked at the shattered remains and then back up at the landing. A ghostly figure now stood there. Focusing, the figure became more cohesive, and he could make out more details. It was male, dressed in old-style clothing, about six foot in height and of average build. Its form was mildly blurred, and the dark eyes in a swarthy complexion returned his gaze. Laughter emanated from its mirthless features. Seconds later the laughter turned demonic, and its features followed suit, turning into a wicked grimace with eyes turning black as coal. A scowling mouth and twisted features transformed it into a demented face from hell. Dark auras now surrounded the being as its true energies manifested.

Mark's defensive barrier instantly slammed into place. Grounding into the earth beneath him, he felt his spirit guides step in close. More like soldiers than the usual spirit guides, they too sensed that battle was imminent. He instinctively raised his hands, and light shot out of them, streaking up the stairs. Almost too fast for the eye to see, they reached the dark spirit, instantaneously wrapping around him, binding him on the spot. With a cry of rage it tried to move. Fully allowing his guides to infuse him with their power, a sense of determination and righteousness flowed through Mark, and he stomped up the stairs towards the dark spirit. Reaching the landing at the top of the stairs he took hold of the restrained dark entity. Struggling against its bonds, it stared at him with undisguised malevolence.

Mark picked it up with a grip around its throat and groin and hoisted it up into the air, its feet thrashing futilely. Too late to realise its plight, it screamed as, with a mighty heave, he threw it down the stairs to waiting guides who firmly took hold of it.

'*See how you like it! Take it away,*' he said to the guides who now held the spirit.

Catching his breath, Mark turned his attention back up the stairs. His senses were now fully attuned, and he could feel other dark spirits around him. How had they escaped his notice till now? While he was tired and distracted, they had lain in wait for him, trying to catch him unawares. They had almost succeeded except for that sixth sense he seemed to possess which had once again saved him.

As he turned left up the second flight of stairs, more dark spirits appeared, and he was accosted from all sides. They were leaching from his aura, trying to gain access within. Mark was in no mood now to be interfered with. Flanked with his two main soldier guides, he took hold of each of them as they appeared, tossing them aside as though they weighed nothing to waiting spiritual hands that took them away to be dealt with.

He strode purposefully up to the second landing and walked into the first bedroom. No sooner had he stepped in than a shoe flew past his head, striking the wall behind him with a large thud. Turning to the source of danger, he focused in the far corner. The energy in the room was dark and electric. An old woman in clothing of the late 1800s appeared in the corner. A dark aura surrounded her, matching the black shawl she had draped over her shoulders. A large, shabby, bilious dark green skirt covered the lower part of her body. Furious at his intrusion, she screamed in rage like a demented banshee. Another shoe appeared in her hand, and she threw it at him, narrowly missing his head as he ducked. He stood upright, and light shot from his hands, binding the raised hand as simultaneously a bedside lamp rose from a nearby bedside cabinet as though from her bidding. Her hand was thrown back and pinned against the wall, and the offending lamp dropped unceremoniously back onto the cabinet with a loud clatter.

Mark stepped forward and swiftly took hold of her in a vice-like grip. Hissing and screaming, the woman glared malevolently at him.

'What do you want?' he said out loud.

Saying nothing, she continued to rail at him, immobile but demented and furious.

'What do you want?' he repeated. 'Why are you here? Who sent you?'

He pulled his head back swiftly, narrowly avoiding her snapping teeth that were vying for his face. Shaking her roughly, he strengthened his grip.

'Behave!' he bellowed.

'This is going nowhere,' he muttered to himself. With an almost casual gesture he turned her towards the waiting spirit workers who dragged her away, kicking and screaming.

Something was going on here. He had been set up, drawn to this house deliberately and ambushed with significant numbers and force. But why?

Had Anya known? Instantly he dismissed the question. She had neither the power nor the ability to arrange this. Indeed, why would she? Had he not been the only one who had helped her in the last couple of years when no other could? He had saved her and her family so many times. There would be no reason for her to turn on him.

So, perhaps she had been forced to help attack him? Again, no. She wasn't capable. Maybe she was an unwitting pawn? This too seemed unlikely. She just wasn't a big enough player in this game, not even in the same league. She was just a victim in all of this.

So who then? Or what?

CHAPTER 23

THE PAINTING

Underworld [noun]: A realm of dark energy existing below us where beings of a more earthy nature exist. All are dark at the moment they exist there, but not all stay dark. The indigenous life forms residing there, however, are all dark matter.

He walked carefully up the remaining stairs but found no other wayward dark spirits. However, a feeling of hostility still permeated throughout the house.

He remembered the ill-feeling painting he'd seen earlier and made his way back down to the lounge. Standing in front of it, Mark stared hard, trying to figure out what was causing his unease. Objects can carry all kinds of negativity. They can be infused with dark energy, have spiritual attachments linked to them, be cursed, or be a focus for black magic or dark spiritual beings. They can even act as a focal point for a gateway between realms. These objects should be handled with extreme care for all too obvious reasons. And they can take any form. Even the most unobtrusive bland object can be the recipient of dark energy.

Mark reached up and lifted the painting off the wall. A feeling of negativity ran through his hands as soon as he touched it. It was rectangular in shape, approximately eighteen inches by twelve inches, and it was deceptively heavy with an ornate dark red wooden frame. As though a valve had been released, dark energy started to pour off it in waves. He tuned in to find its source, and the answer was soon forthcoming.

As he looked into the painting with his spirit eyes, the canvas became three dimensional in appearance as a dark opening appeared that reached down into a seamless, depthless tunnel. This was a gateway to one of the underworld levels! An entity of some kind had been using the picture as its gateway, controlling it and allowing entry and exit between realms. That's how so many dark spirits had come into one place at one time! This was the gateway from whence they came. It had to be closed before more dark spirits crossed over, and it had to be closed now!

Mark mentally summoned a dark lord from the underworld to take back control of the gateway and its wayward minions. Moments later one appeared at his side. It was more than seven feet high, dark and foreboding. The demonic being stepped up to the painting and took hold of the gateway on either side with taloned hands. Lesser elemental beings appeared within, taking their positions inside the opening and securing the perimeter. The dark lord stepped into the gateway and dropped into the abyss, dragging the outer edges of the gateway with it. Instantly it sealed shut, and all that could now be seen was the original flat Hispanic painting.

Now that the gateway had been closed, Mark knew what had to be done next. To prevent this painting ever being used in such a way again, it needed to be destroyed. And there was only one sure way you could guarantee that. It had to be burnt.

Mark carried the painting into the back garden, put it down on the paving slabs outside, and walked back into the kitchen. After a few moments hunting around, he found some matches and lighter fuel in one of the cupboards. Armed with these tools, he strode back into the garden, uncapping the lighter fuel as he went. He poured copious amounts of the fluid onto the painting, covering it from edge to edge. The smell of liquid gas fumes filled his nostrils. He took out two matches and struck them alight, placing the lit matches back into the full box. The box flared into life with a flash of chemical heat and light, and he tossed it onto the saturated painting, which burst into flames as the matches struck and caught the lighter fuel. Within moments the painting was a mini inferno, flames licking hungrily at the old wood and canvas backing.

As he watched the flames dance and do their job, Mark whispered to the universe.

'I transmute this into positive energy and close this gateway for ever.'

'Done' echoed in his mind.

And only ashes were left.

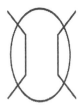

CHAPTER 24

THE BASEMENT

Archdemon [noun]: The archangel's counterpart. A highly evolved and ancient consciousness that controls demons and other dark matter beings. Like their opposites, they rarely incarnate fully on the earth plane other than as energy.

As he stood and reflected, Mark knew there was something still amiss. Who or what was behind all this? A thought entered his mind. *'The Basement. I need to check that out.'* Seconds later he found himself in the kitchen at the top of the staircase that led down into the basement. Dark and gloomy, it was far from inviting.

He flicked on the light switch, and the room below became visible, though its single bulb cast only sparse illumination. He slowly descended. The atmosphere became eerily quiet as he reached the last couple of steps, pausing on the final one. Soaking up the now decidedly hostile feeling in the basement, he looked around as he stepped into the room proper. He turned the corner of the banister. The large double bed was still in situ, pushed against the far wall. A rug adorned the floor in front. Strangely, he hadn't noticed this before. Woven with what appeared to be natural fibres, mainly browns, creams, and reds, it formed a strange mosaic pattern that spiralled down in a circular motion towards the centre, like a funnel.

He glanced behind him at the scattering of furniture, but all was motionless. *Everything* was motionless. The hairs stood up on the back of his neck as an unnatural silence filled the room. Only the sound of his deep rhythmic breathing could be heard.

Suddenly he sensed a stirring in the air behind him. It was just a whisper, but it was all the warning he needed. He spun on his heel as a dark elemental stepped out from the shadowy depths of the corner behind him. It moved towards him at speed, appearing as though from the walls itself. Mark had mere moments to react, but he was faster. His hands rose up in a flash, and light sped out in an instant, smiting it straight in the chest, checking its forward motion with a jolt.

Raising a wall of brilliant gold light in front of him, Mark pushed the entity back toward the corner and pinned it there. With a roar of rage, it beat uselessly against the impenetrable wall of light. Its gaping maw showed small fangs dripping spittle. He could see now that it was a soldier elemental, one who would work for a higher dark being from the underworld. Its limbs were disjointed with a hard exoskeleton surrounding its body. Long legs sat below a bulging thorax, as its elongated arms hammered against the wall of light. Its strength was prodigious, and the constant battering of the shield he'd erected was draining. He wouldn't be able to hold it forever.

'What do you want?' he asked out loud.

'*Your death*!' it replied in his mind.

'Who sent you?'

Silence was his reply, while the relentless pounding assault against his shield increased. Waves of light rippled out from the points of impact, but it held firm.

'Who sent you? He asked again with more intensity.

It refused to answer, and a trickle of sweat ran down his cheek with the effort of maintaining his shield. This was getting nowhere. He needed to send it back whence it came from soon. This wasn't the main entity in charge. It was just a soldier.

With a summoning thought, a black circular gateway opened up behind the entity, and two dark beings rose up from its inky depths. Taking an arm each, they dragged the hapless elemental down into the abyss, and the gateway snapped shut. Dropping his shield, Mark took a deep breath.

He was drained but remained on high alert. Something was still wrong here. The soldier elemental was gone, but it just felt … wrong.

Looking around, he could see nothing. His guides stepped in close, flanking his shoulders. Others were close by, ready to do his bidding in an instant. His eyes flicked around the basement. They stopped at the rug as they glanced over it. Squinting in the gloom to try and see better, he thought he detected a slight disturbance in the air. He stared hard for a few seconds to confirm it. A slight ripple was forming millimetres above the carpet. It felt like watching a heat wave coming off a hot surface in the distance. He suddenly felt cold and rubbed his arms as the surrounding temperature dropped dramatically, and his breath came out in large clouds of steam. The rug became distorted as the air appeared to swirl around and the ripples became waves.

His body involuntarily shivered as he watched the space where the rug had been transform into a big black bottomless hole. A gateway! But unlike any he would summon! It was larger and deeper, and evil rose from inside. Taloned claws appeared over the edge, and a dark brown leathery skull with pointed ears followed as a dark being of immense power hauled itself out of the gateway.

Mark took a step back. He knew he was in serious danger. This was the being that was in control, and it was far more powerful than anything from the underworld he had come across before.

An elongated muzzle with long fangs protruded from what would be called its mouth. It snarled. Its huge broad shoulders appeared as it started to lever itself out of the gateway. One taloned foot gained purchase, and bulging thighs drove it fully out and into the basement. Pure evil emanated from it in waves, and Mark was forced to take another involuntary step back. Stunned at what he was seeing, his shields swiftly slammed down about him and his solider guides took up flanking positions.

Red flaming eyes scanned the basement till they finally locked on his own. Mocking laughter poured from deep within the dark lord's huge barrel-like chest. Muscle bulged wherever you looked, and its stomach heaved as it laughed humourlessly.

'So now you find me,' it said in a deep inhuman voice.

'Who are you?' Mark's voice was steady. A confidence came through despite the very real danger he knew he was in right now.

'My true name you couldn't pronounce in your tongue, but by some I am known as Belthazar.'

Thinking quickly, he knew he had heard this name before. Belthazar was an archdemon, and although he'd never seen him, Mark had no doubt that he was exactly who he said he was.

Mark swore under his breath. He needed to think fast. He needed help—and fast! A taloned hand reached out and touched his shield, testing it. Sparks flew off, but the shield held.

'What do you want? Why have you come?'

Belthazar paused before he answered. 'Debts must be paid, inconveniences removed. You're just a pawn who got in the way. A fly in the ointment, you could say.' He gave a hollow laugh again. 'There are things going on you can't possibly comprehend.'

'Really? Try me.'

'Enough talk!' Belthazar bellowed, and the room shook with his power. 'Time for you to go, little man.' Menacingly, he took a step forward.

Mark intensified his shield, bracing himself as he raised his spiritual voice, shouting out to the heavens.

'*Michael! I need you!*'

Within an instant, a feeling of peace flooded through his very core, and a huge blue presence appeared alongside him. Without turning his head to see, he already knew who had arrived. Archangel Michael stood there, resplendent in bright silver armour, his hand casually resting on his long glowing blue sword. He looked across at his opposite, the archdemon.

Belthazar froze. His forward motion towards Mark stopped dead.

'So the puppy has called his master. Very clever. Very wise.'

For what seemed like an eternity to Mark, they looked across the room at each other. Their eyes were locked, and Mark was all but forgotten. The tension rose, and the very air crackled about them with fiery energy.

'Well? said Michael, 'What's it to be, Belthazar? Are you finally ready to challenge me?'

Balthazar leant forward, tense, and for a second it looked as though he was going to attack. Then he leant back and relaxed.

'Not today. There will be other times, Michael. See to your puppy.'

With that, he stepped back over his gateway to the underworld. He dropped down into its depths and vanished, along with any trace that either he or the gateway had ever existed.

Mark let out an explosive breath that he hadn't even realised he'd been holding and turned to face Michael.

'Thank you,' he said with genuine gratitude.

'You're welcome. That was never your fight. We were aware of a disturbance in the ether, but it wasn't till you called out that I knew exactly where and what,' he said with a slight smile.

'So it's over now?'

'For now, yes. But there will be other battles. You will be called upon again.'

'What's been happening here?'

'There is a bigger picture, a universal one, one in which you seem to have a part. For now, though, you are safe. Everything is as it should be.'

He turned as though to leave but turned back.

'You did well,' he said, smiling. Benevolence radiated from him, and Mark felt peace and love wash through his entire being.

And Michael vanished.

With a sigh, Mark looked around. He was exhausted and had no desire to stay here any longer. Everything had slotted into place, and the immediate questions had been answered. All was right in the world for now. And that's all he could ask for.

It was time to go home.

CHAPTER 25

TRAINING COMPLETED

Red Shaman, Abatheer and Malek stood in the clouds, intent observers of goings on below. They watched three dark forms vanish from the hut, streaming up into the sky above, changing colour and shape as they morphed back into Light Beings of their Order.

'*Well that was a success, I'd say,*' Abatheer proclaimed.

Malek nodded.

Both looked at Red Shaman. They knew the final decision rested with him, and they were not about to interrupt his musings. Their role was to advise, help, and support only. Their views were largely academic, both as to the scenario at hand and their future position of elevation.

'*Indeed, he has done well. As have we. Send our thanks to the three earlier. They completed their tasks with aplomb and should be rewarded.*'

Abatheer and Malek exchanged glances. It was unusual for Red Shaman to be so benign. He must be pleased with events indeed, they both thought.

Abatheer breathed a silent sigh of relief. '*Of course, it shall be done as you wish.*'

Red Shaman looked up, glancing from one to the other. '*You've performed well. I'm pleased with both of you.*' An unexpected smile graced his normally serious features. '*Maybe now we'll receive* a moment of peace before the next phase. *Right after we've made our reports, that is. Records must be kept for the Halls of Akasha, and all must be in order.*'

With that, Abatheer and Malek vanished, leaving a pensive Red Shaman behind.

All was as it should be. He understood this was just one stage in a never-ending cycle of universal evolvement across the realms. Always moving. Changing with the ebb and flow of time across the universe. Both known and unknown.

But there was one last test to be completed, and *that* was put in place eons ago. And for once it was out of his hands. With a shrug of his shoulders, Red Shaman also vanished to a place never seen by human eyes—or by too many others, for that matter.

CHAPTER 26

BACK TO THE LIGHT

Humangel [noun]: A wingless angel of the lower ranks, sent down to the earth plane at times of struggle and strife. While rare in the early days, their presence nowadays was pretty much permanent. Few of them know who they really are or what their exact purpose is.

The boy, the three witch doctors, and the spirit demons that had been expelled from the earth plane by Mark had been studying together for some time now. They formed their own soul group and were being taught by an assemblage of seven angels. The negative energies they had been absorbing on the earth plane had been completely neutralised upon their arrival in the reprocessing areas of the Akashic Halls. They were at peace at last.

For the first few lessons, they reviewed their actions and came to understand their role. Latterly, they had been taught how to neutralise energies just like themselves.

For some, their mission on earth had lasted thousands of years; for others just a few hundred. They learned that they were necessary 'sinks' for negative energy generated by humans. They absorbed the negative detritus that was generated by billions of human minds—feelings of hate and loathing, buckets of guilt, and vats full of fear. When any human harboured such thoughts, they leaked out into the air. If they weren't mopped up, the earth plane would be toxic to life as the earthlings knew it. Earth was actually one of the more successful planets in the cosmos. The managing angels had at last got the balance about right. The designs of the archangels were working.

Some sensitive souls on the earth plane, like Anya, were naturally soft targets for such energies. With low self-esteem and lack of self-worth, the Anyas of the world draw these energies to them.

This was all part of soul contracts pre-agreed in the other Halls of Akasha. In each incarnation, some souls chose to play victim, others aggressors, and others healers. The accumulated learnings across time added to the collective thought pool.

So after a month or so of teachings and reprogramming for the group, it was time for the next phase of their journey. (Incidentally, a week in heaven lasts for a nanosecond and an aeon both at the same time.)

The ex-demons were assembled together and told to surround the boy. In turn, the seven angels surrounded the group. The angels breathed on them in synchronicity, and they fused into the boy as one cohesive entity.

'*We baptise you Mark,*' said the leader of the angels. '*You are to return to the earth plane in 1966. Your father is a policeman, and this will be your profession too.*'

'*What is my purpose?*' asked the boy.

'*Simply to learn and to return with what you find.*'

AUTHOR'S NOTE

Since the beginning of time there has been the eternal battle between Light and Dark, both vying for supremacy. In fact, this is how creation occurs. If all was dark, we would stagnate. If all was light, we would stagnate. Creation precedes this conflict, this light and dark mix. We learn and grow from our experiences both pleasant and unpleasant. Without these experiences we would atrophy into some mundane existence of mediocrity at best.

So look at this as the way of the universe, the way it continues to grow and evolve. We humans are Light Beings at our core. We should always strive to be at peace and harmony with each other and especially with ourselves, combating the dark around us in so many forms. Even simple thought forms offered by another in emotional moments can emit massive negative energy. So be mindful of your thoughts and keep looking for your peace within—your inner light, your harmony. And be tempted not by the dark. That is *our* role in this universe. Most of us anyway.

ABOUT THE AUTHOR

David Walther was born in West London. His early career was spent serving in various roles in the public sector.

In 1996 David began studying Hua Tuo Qi Gong, a rarer form of self-healing Qi Gong, under a Chinese master who had moved to England from China. This was his first introduction into Chi energy. At first this came in the form of self-healing from Qi Gong, but it wasn't long before David was able to transmit Chi himself.

In 2006 David started his spiritual journey in earnest, learning from many teachers, and was fast-tracked by spirit. This enabled him to help others to greater effect with an expanding repertoire of abilities, which are still continuously growing and improving. Now living in Surrey, David continues to learn and evolve whilst teaching and helping others.

Find out more about David and his work here: www.davidwalther.co

WRITTEN BY
DAVID WALTHER

Printed in Great Britain
by Amazon